Social Reform Movements to Protect
America's Vulnerable 1830–1940

WOMEN &
CHILDREN
First

Edited by David J. Rothman and
Sheila M. Rothman

A Garland Series

THE CARE OF THE UNMARRIED MOTHER

Robert South Barrett

Garland Publishing, Inc.
New York & London
1987

For a complete list of the titles in this series
see the final pages of this volume.

This facsimile has been made from a copy in the Library of Congress.

Library of Congress Cataloging-in-Publication Data

Barrett, Robert South, 1877–1959.
 The care of the unmarried mother.

 (Women & children first)
 Reprint. Originally published: Alexandria, Va. : s.n., 1929.
 Includes index.
 1. Unmarried mothers—Services for—United States.   2. Il-
legitimacy—United States.   I. Title.   II. Series.
 HV700.5.B37   1987   362.8′392′0973   87-19748
 ISBN 0-8240-7651-6 (alk. paper)

The volumes in this series are printed on
acid-free, 250-year-life paper.

Printed in the United States of America

DR. KATE WALLER BARRETT (1858-1925)
"The Mother of Girls"

Portrait in American Legion Headquarters, Indianapolis

THE CARE

OF THE

UNMARRIED MOTHER

By

ROBERT SOUTH BARRETT

President of the National Florence Crittenton Mission

1929

ALEXANDRIA, VIRGINIA

To the hundreds of thousands of girls in the United States whose devotion to their children has brought them through the humiliating shadows of unmarried motherhood to the highest realization of the ideals of womanhood, this book is affectionately dedicated.

PREFACE

The question of the unmarried mother is one of the most important social problems of the present day, but despite the large number of individuals and agencies who are interested in her welfare, there is a dearth of printed material dealing with her problems. This book has been prepared to remedy that defect. It is largely the result of the investigations of my mother, the late Dr. Kate Waller Barrett, of Alexandria, Va., who devoted nearly fifty years to the subject. She was one of the pioneers of the work in this country and lived to see a complete change in the attitude of the enlightened public toward the girl who makes a misstep that leads to the birth of a child out of wedlock.

In addition to personal contact with Dr. Barrett during her life, and access to her letters and addresses, the writer had available the following sources of information:

1. The opinion on practically all of the factors involved of sixty officials of maternity homes located in every section of the United States, based on their study and observation of over 50,000 cases of unmarried mothers who have been under their care during the past 25 years.

2. An examination and analysis of nearly 10,000 case records of maternity homes in large and small cities of the United States with an effort to put a proper valuation upon the ability and trustworthiness of the person who made the investigation.

3. Individual surveys made in different cities of the United States and largely based on case records, a number of which have never been printed.

4. A study during the past ten years of the personal and mental characteristics as well as the records of nearly a thousand girls who have been inmates of Ivakota Farms, Fairfax County, Va., practically all of whom were sex delinquents.

The writer desires to express his appreciation for the assistance received in preparing this work to the following persons: To Mr. Otto Wilson, of Washington, D. C., for research work in securing data on illegitimacy and compiling the chapter on the legal side of the question; to Dr. Ernst Freund, of the University of Chicago, for revision of the chapter on illegitimacy laws, which was largely taken from his book on this subject; to Mr. Clarence R. Preston, executive secretary of the Florence Crittenton League of Compassion of Boston, for his valuable suggestions; and to Dr. George B. Mangold, of the University of Southern California, for permission to use the introduction taken from his book, "Children Born Out of Wedlock." Material from the Federal Children's Bureau, especially its handbook on institutions for children, has been freely used. In Chapter Two some of the conclusions, as well as the language, have been taken from Dr. Kammerer's book, "The Unmarried Mother."

ROBERT S. BARRETT.

TABLE OF CONTENTS

INTRODUCTION

Not until a few years ago was it possible to discuss sex problems in public and before mixed gatherings. The topic of illegitimacy was tabooed and people dared to talk only in whispers about evidence of immorality and vice. Even today such words as "prostitute," "illegitimate," "bastard" and similar expressions can with difficulty find a place in our daily newspapers. Nevertheless, a tremendous change has taken place in the popular mind. Everywhere individuals are beginning to speak more freely on some of these forbidden subjects. Social workers in particular have recognized the need of sound public opinion in order that some advance might be made in the solution of sex problems. Investigations of various kinds have therefore been instituted and a pamphlet literature on illegitimacy and allied topics has begun to accumulate. The great world war has accentuated the problem. In Europe the volume of illegitimacy is dangerously great; moreover, with the outbreak of the war, motives, impulses and tendencies were liberated which have, no doubt, increased the irregular relations which before were already altogether too common. Our own illegitimacy rate has been rather low and the problem as a whole has not given the social worker much serious concern. However, certain social agencies have been forced to deal with the unmarried mother and her friendless child and have begun to realize the growing gravity of conditions in the United States. Furthermore, the entrance of our country into the great struggle between democracy and autocracy focused the eyes of thousands, who had not thought of the problem before, on the moral dangers which usually accompany the abnormal functioning of so large a proportion of the population. Many social agencies have tried to prepare themselves to meet the new situation and an active campaign has been organized among young women to insure their moral protection.

It is to be hoped that measures of this kind will prevent any considerable increase in the amount of illegitimacy but whatever be the results without doubt attention has been called to this question in so emphatic a way that the lesson will never be forgotten and as a consequence there will develop a new and saner program for the care of the illegitimate child.

In the past the world has always tolerated a double standard of morals. This has especially oppressed the sex that could not defend itself in a contest of physical powers. The male has usually been the aggressive, and the female the passive sex. Nevertheless, gross deviations by the former from the path of sex rectitude have received but little condemnation, while a slight error of woman has usually been visited with the swiftest and most condign punishment. The original sex standards were largely a man-made product. Woman had but little share in shaping these standards and she accepted them without much protest. Eventually she applied them in most rigid manner and as a consequence the so-called fallen woman has become an outcast while the equally guilty man has remained in good social standing.

Man has long tried to teach woman the beauty of woman's virtue. The old Roman father plunged his knife into his daughter's heart rather than see her virtue stained. Jacob's sons spoiled a city because their sister sold her virtue to Shechem. The ancient German jealously guarded the virtue of his daughters and taught them the lesson of purity; wherever Teutonic ideals have taken root, chastity of woman has become almost as dear as life itself.

Society has always struggled with the self-centered motives of individuals and has found it especially difficult to temper the selfishness of the male. The noble Roman did not shrink at the thought of destroying the virtue of a barbarian's daughter or even of a helpless Roman woman. Israel's sons did not respect the virtue of Canaan's daughters. The German was not as true to his neighbor's daughter as to his own. Had the male applied to himself a small part of the austere morals he demanded of the other sex, our history would tell a different story and our morals would be of different character. But the coercion which man exercised was never matched by a similar coercion from woman, and the standards of today condone in man what they hold unpardonable in woman. The unmarried mother silently bore the burden of her transgressions and as an outcast completed a life full of despair. Few were left to mourn her loss or departure. Her sins had blackened her soul beyond cleansing and no one could afford to suffer the degradation which companionship with her would inevitably impose. Dishonored, she sank into a forgotten grave.

In recent years, however, her claims on life and on human compassion have gradually received a new consideration. Instead of being branded with the scarlet letter on her breast and placed in the pillory on the public square, she has in some cases obtained a second opportunity and, occasionally, fair treatment. In literature, maternity unsanctioned by the law or the church has pleaded for the mercy that ennobles the human breast, and gradually in law the unmarried mother has gained new rights. Sentiment, the supreme court of public opinion, however, has not reversed its decision nor seriously modified its implications and today the forbidden step still leads to human desolation and the wilderness of buried hope. And yet, not entirely. The dawn of a new day is at hand and is slowly giving way to justice. This movement has compelled men to become introspective. Is not sin equally black whether committed by male or female? Has sin a sex? Is it peculiar to woman? Questions such as these haunt virtuous and socially minded men to whom the unfairness of today makes its invincible appeal, and to whom the bitterness that envelops a betrayed woman's soul engenders a sense of outraged justice. Slowly, men will rise above themselves and say "we too have sinned." Why do we throw stones? Slowly, men begin to see the injustice which ruins one sex but excuses the other. Accordingly, a change is gradually taking place which will not make morality among women less desirable, although a greater opportunity for restoration to society will be given, but which will subject the sexually immoral male to such disgrace and reprobation that the humiliation will act as a powerful deterrent.

In other words, moral standards among women are not to be lowered, but standards among men will rise until the two intersect and a common ground will be reached. The increased rights and opportunities of woman are partly responsible for this movement. When woman was unfit for education, for professional life, for public service, and was used chiefly as a beast of burden, for rearing children and for sex gratification, her rights were precariously few. But the gradual emancipation of women brings with it not only a release from galling handicaps in industry, science and education, but it also forces a reconsideration of the double standard of morals.

The social wrong of today lies not so much in the severe penalty imposed upon the offending woman, but on the comparative immunity granted the more blameworthy men. The young man falls in love with a virtuous girl; they promise to marry; she is persuaded to yield her body; he repudiates the woman he has deceived and her maternity is buried in disgrace. She becomes an outcast, his sin is soon forgotten; he marries another woman or ruins some fresh and innocent girl. Is it any wonder that in this age of unrest, when justice is being enthroned, that the women denounce a system which treats them so harshly and relentlessly?

It is evident that public sentiment concerning illegitimacy has been shaped by the operation of several important factors. The female sex must bear the young. Woman must carry the physical evidences of approaching maternity and cannot hide the evidence of her shame. The finger can always be pointed at her because her guilt cannot remain undiscovered, but the equally guilty man can easily escape, since no one but the unfortunate woman herself knows his identity. Pregnancy and child birth label the woman. Next follows the handicap of caring for the child or the disagreeable task of disposing of it. Illegitimacy, therefore, imposes on woman a special burden and her marriageability, as well as economic and social usefulness, is affected thereby.

Consequently, the natural and almost inevitable effect of illegitimacy has been disgrace to woman. Undoubtedly this result is partly responsible for the high standards applied to women both by themselves and the opposite sex. If immorality is so baneful in its physiological and economic consequences, then it is most unsocial and cannot be too strongly condemned. The physiology of sex is, therefore, one of the natural, but not necessarily persistent, causes of a double standard of morals. The handicaps of a woman with her baby, the comparative immorality, the difficulty in maintaining a livelihood and other correlated conditions have proven a great disadvantage.

The second factor was the physical superiority and greater mobility of man. It was difficult to impose penalties on man as it was almost impossible to prove paternity; hence, few men would be disgraced and the disgrace that was attached to a man was soon forgotten. He did not carry with him the evidences of his misconduct. People were not constantly reminded of his sin; and therefore an ignorant community soon forgot to associate a certain man with the offense and its consequences. Or a guilty man might flee to some distant locality and begin life anew without being followed by public knowledge of his misdeeds. Without the physical brand of wrongdoing on his person his escape from responsibility has been comparatively easy.

That the double standard of today is, in part at least, the natural outcome of utilitarian conditions that constantly shape morals is without question. In a society where foresight was slight, solidarity largely absent, and conscious planning in a primitive state, the double standard arose as the inevitable result of the requisites of social survival and individual happiness. Consequently, law and religion both sanctioned the differences that existed in the respective treatment of offending men and women. The disparity of conditions in the twentieth century is a survival of the coercion of the ages. It represents the codified results of past experience and the conservation of a principle that once protected women from the tendency to practice unlawful sex relations.

In the light of history shall we then say that the double standard must remain for all time? Is it not true that the rights and opportunities of women have always been subordinated to those of men? Yet the woman's movement has in less than one hundred years gained for women results more remarkable than has been achieved in all previous history. Has not the superstition that woman must be subordinated and discriminated against been largely destroyed? Has woman not gained the right to education, to a professional career, to voluntary celibacy, to greater freedom of movement, to greater privileges before the law, and, in some countries, to the right to participate in the affairs of government and to a living wage? Without doubt, the social and political emancipation of women is proceeding at a most rapid rate although the gains are all of comparatively recent time. The difference in standards of morals is evidently a case in sex discrimination and is not the only form of discrimination that has existed. The existence from time immemorial of other differences has not proven their basic or inherent character. In fact, many of these are already destroyed. We cannot, therefore, conclude on the basis of analogy that the double standard of morals is either ineradicable or inevitable. Its social coercion may not be more persuasive than that of other extinct forms of discrimination.

In this age when all forms of injustice are attacked and, if possible, reduced or destroyed, the double standard of morals must submit to a new examination of its merits, and if not based on fundamental conditions of social welfare, its appeal will fail. Illegitimacy must always bear more heavily on women than on men since the fundamental nature of maleness and femaleness necessitates this difference. If the individual effect were the true basis for the moral standard, then the exactions demanded of woman must be more severe than the requirements imposed on men. The social effect, however, is the more important influence and must determine standards. Is our social welfare best promoted by a uniform standard or by one that discriminates against woman? Do the factors that once operated to produce a dual standard still continue in force? Or have they been replaced by new considerations? One factor of great importance cannot be passed over without emphasis on its far-reaching influence. It is the power of human passion. Is it equal in the sexes or unequal? If equal, then why the great excess of male immorality? If unequal, is the difference inherent or due to conditions that can be modified? The author does not propose to offer the last word on this subject. He does not insist that it has a tremendous bearing on the problems of a single standard of morals. So-called virtue is of two varieties; that which results in good actions, no temptations to evil being present, and that which overcomes temptation and triumphantly presents the good. To what extent is the virtue of woman a victory of mind over body? To what extent in man? This important question is receiving much attention today, and advanced advocates of social hygiene insist that "sex necessity" is false doctrine and that perfect continence is possible. This argument is, of course, advanced to apply to the great bulk of males, to all except a few who are perverts. That a large proportion of men are moral is undoubtedly true, but the problem relates itself to those, whether a minority or the majority, who have not remained moral. Are they capable of self-restraint? If so, even though it be more difficult than in the case of woman, incontinence can be wiped out and illegitimacy and prostitution eliminated. A higher ideal will inevitably bring severer condemnation on the offending male and a nearer approach to a uniform standard of morals. Greater self-control, increased capacity for self-control and improved social conditions will surely work in the direction of a single standard of morals.

More and more the welfare of humanity must be expressed in terms of mental joy and satisfaction. With the increasing recognition of woman's right to happiness it depends in greater measure than ever before on high ideals and good morals. In the near future women will not overlook immorality among their male friends and finally marry sexually tainted men. The woman of tomorrow cannot respect the man "with a past." Happy homes cannot be founded on a dual standard. So long as women were ignorant, the menace to the homes was slight, but with the intellectual emancipation of women must come the collapse of the old system and the introduction of an equality which will force men to standards similar to those men have enforced on women.

The highest form of mutual respect cannot exist where dual standards are maintained. Again, the attitude of parents toward children is more wholesome when the parents thoroughly respect each other. Sons will receive better guidance and daughters will be taught to demand clean companions. Wifehood, motherhood and childhood all plead for a uniform level of morals.

Decades must pass, however, before the attitude toward men will be identical with that toward women. But so long as it differs, so long men are logically compelled to regard illegitimacy, immorality and prostitution as tolerable, and their female victims as inevitable sacrifices to the lust of men. Nevertheless, logic does not control and immoral women are reviled and become social outcasts. If the double standard is necessary then these women should receive the respect due to any group that performs a public service.

That the social consequences of illegitimacy are disastrous admits of no serious doubt. That men are more aggressive than women and also more blameworthy is, furthermore, true. From the social point of view, man as the co-partner and aggressor is the greater offender and his condemnation should be the more severe. His actions cannot be extenuated; and a stern standard of morals must be imposed in order that deterrent effects may be realized. Society must make demands proportionate to the conditions. Therefore the standard of morals should bear more heavily on men than on women, although the converse is at present the case.

The sex instinct is present in every normal man and woman. The legal opportunity for that instinct to function should be gained by all persons some time in life; that is, marriage should be within the range of all normal people. The unmarried, whether men or women, must, to remain moral, restrain their sex impulses. To do this their energies and activities must be directed into other channels and the effect of such diversion must overcome the latent but ever present impulse of sex.

No one has yet informed the world of the width of the gap between the normal impulse in man and in woman. Yet, our whole program of social hygiene, sex education and treatment of sexual offenses depends on the answer of this question. Have we ever stopped to realize the effect on mind and sex impulse of the slush and filth with which a large proportion of young boys are bespattered? Have we ever attempted to weigh the effect of the false ideals taught to our youth, of the "manliness" of sex immorality; of the environment and coercive habits of adolescence and young manhood? Suppose the exact environment of the young girls and women with its ban on the individual right of self-expression, of emotion and sex impulse were imposed on the male sex, what would be the effect?

On the other hand, if our young girls should hear the language and thoughts expressed before the youth of our land would not an awakening of sex consciousness follow, the grave consequences of which would appall the world? Even now we find among the neglected and delinquent girls that appear before our juvenile courts an astounding mass of immorality. Is the girl who lives with her family in a single room, where sex faces her constantly, made sexually precocious, or do her sex instincts slumber on as in the case of many "sheltered" girls? There is the utmost need of an exhaustive case study made by competent persons of one or two thousand young women capable of interpreting themselves and of linking sex instinct with other emotions and impulses. The sexuality of the unmarried woman is hid under a bushel. She dares not disclose it, yet it surely must be there, and only too often the dread fact of illegitimacy, prostitution or immorality reveals a condition which should have received rational attention instead of being shunned and disdained because of a mock modesty. The woman has yet to appear who will write truthfully and courageously and constructively about her sex and who will open the eyes of the world to the sex life of women. Yet without such knowledge, we cannot meet our problems and solve them. We can only guess and then work in darkness. Nor has the man presented himself who has weighed the innate and acquired sex impulses of man and woman and who has given us an adequate basis for a social program. The physician and physiologist should face this question fearlessly and not for the sake of developing some particular propaganda whether good or bad. The social worker should strive to attain fundamentals. It does not necessarily follow that because a young woman has been corrupted, laws punishing the guilty man should be regarded as a solution of the problem. Nor must we assume that the coarse woman of the street is an original source of corruption and that to punish her solves a problem. The moralist has much to learn about sex life. The time to put on moral blinkers or to ignore facts, after the fashion of the ostrich, has passed. We need to get upon the solid earth, then determine our latitude and ascertain our whereabouts. When the physiologist, the moralist, the lawmaker and the social worker have properly constructed their fortress of fundamental facts, then the task of destroying the various sexual sins can be undertaken in real earnest and some measure of success will be assured. Much time will elapse before this goal will be attained. Meanwhile, a program of amelioration must be carried out; hope restored to women who are hopeless; and a burden placed on the shoulders of both the man and the woman who are partners in an offense against themselves and a sin against society.

The social consequences of illegitimacy are most disastrous. Both sexes are indispensable to the consummation of the offense. The child is innocent and to penalize him represents a vicarious sacrifice such as is borne by no other group of unfortunates throughout the world. It is a wrong with perhaps no extenuating circumstances. It is impossible to believe that injustice to innocent children is necessary in order to compel men and women to perform their moral obligations and to live morally.

To penalize woman, to disgrace her irretrievably, especially in view of the social responsibility for her downfall, resembles torturing an animal and then punishing it for its writhing. Woman is partly to blame and must bear her part of the burden, but she must not be crushed. Without the hope of moral rehabilitation the human being sinks to the level of brute creation and loses every fine instinct that characterizes her as human. In our theories of penology we have advanced sufficiently to reject entirely punishment for the mere sake of justice, to consider its deterrent qualities of minor importance and to make a program of rehabilitation the chief consideration. Not so, however, in the case of illegitimacy. Punishment is drastic and reform hardly attempted.

As far as they relate to men, our laws are almost helpless and public opinion as expressed in the acts of attorneys, judges and juries still more so. The promotion of social welfare requires equal responsibility of the male with the female for their illegitimate offspring. The past emphasis on moral responsibility does not meet the situation. The blame attached has been so light and society has been so forgiving that deterrent effects have hardly been realized. That public action must produce such effects is unquestioned. Probably results can be most easily achieved by means of enforcing drastic financial responsibility for illegitimate children. The Napoleonic Code prohibits inquiry into the paternity of such children and several European countres are still under the spell of this iniquitous point of view. Some American states likewise refuse to attach any responsibility to the putative father. This is most unjust if it is true that men and women should be accorded equal treatment. There should be full inquiry ino the paternity of all illegitimate children, and then paternal responsibility should be imposed. The treatment of illegitimacy must be made to accord with the principles that determine our social welfare.

The attitude toward child, mother and father must be fixed by this consideration. All laws and methods of punishment or treatment must be able to answer the question, do they work toward the highest moral and social welfare of society? Judged from this standpoint there can be but little doubt that disabilities placed on children are ineffective deterents and hardly promote morals. The energetic handling of father and mother, however, should gain results, especially if accomplished in such a manner as will discourage a dual standard of morals and the tradition that girls are the legitimate prey of men anxious to sow a few wild oats. When we will really apply ourselves earnestly and fearlessly to this question we will, no doubt, discover that ignorance and false teaching are such decisive factors that preventive work will soon outstrip corrective work. That will be a happy consummation of our efforts; for it will reduce to a minimum the initial sorrow and suffering as well as the amount of subsequent corrective work. It is toward these ends that the social reformers must bend their energies.

GEORGE B. MANGOLD.

University of Southern California,
Los Angeles, Calif.

CHAPTER ONE

THE UNMARRIED MOTHER IN THE UNITED STATES

In order to plan an intelligent organized effort to aid all un-married mothers in the United States who require assistance from either public funds or private philanthropic agencies, it is necessary to secure some reasonably close estimate of the extent of illegitimacy and some knowledge of the circumstancs surrounding its occurrence.

When we attempt to block out a field of action we find that it is determined first by the actual number of illegitimate births in the country in a given year, and second by the proportion of the unmarried mothers who need to be and can be reached. Not everyone needs our help. Of those who do a number live in more or less inaccessible districts where it is difficult either for agencies to reach them, or for them to come to the agencies. With limited resources the wise policy would seem to be for agencies to concern themselves primarily with those who can be most effectively helped, and then to extend their activities to cover as far as possible the cases which may be termed, geo-graphically and otherwise, "outlying" cases.

EXTENT OF ILLEGITIMACY

For the present the extent of illegitimacy in the United States can only be estimated. No official figures covering the whole country are compiled. It is stated as a generally ac-cepted fact that the illegitimacy rate in the United States is lower than in most other large countries, and much lower than in Denmark, Germany, and other countries of western Europe. How far this difference is to be ascribed to a looser system of reporting these births is yet to be determined. Figures, however, which may be considered as reasonably accurate, at least as compared with earlier data, have been compiled for the larger part of the country and are as follows:

ILLEGITIMATE BIRTHS IN REGISTRATION AREA[2] OF UNITED STATES

Area and Color	1924	1925	1926
Arizona	(2)	(2)	142
Connecticut	400	409	417
Delaware	150	222	206
District of Columbia			
Total	573	533	558
White	116	98	120
Colored	457	435	438
Florida			
Total	1,281	1,264	1,398
White	265	279	333
Colored	1,016	985	1,065
Idaho	(2)	(2)	95
Illinois	1,854	2,047	2,061
Indiana	872	840	856
Iowa	760	768	645
Kansas	456	434	484
Kentucky			
Total	1,139	1,264	1,147
White	720	807	709
Colored	419	457	438
Maine	365	398	373
Maryland			
Total	1,888	1,798	1,799
White	541	536	491
Colored	1,347	1,262	1,308
Michigan	1,590	1,617	1,784
Minnesota	1,030	1,000	1,006
Mississippi			
Total	2,864	3,345	3,677
White	193	233	240
Colored	2,671	3,112	3,437
Montana	148	124	135
Nebraska	420	450	494
New Hampshire	117	123	115
New Jersey	1,086	1,068	1,003
New York	2,876	2,974	2,891

North Carolina			
Total	4,853	4,775	4,932
White	1,019	1,124	1,111
Colored	3,834	3,651	3,821
North Dakota	253	269	268
Ohio	2,249	2,268	2,352
Oregon	228	201	206
Pennsylvania	5,213	5,199	4,813
Rhode Island	253	246	226
South Carolina			
Total	4,060	(3)	(3)
White	518	(3)	(3)
Colored	3,542	(3)	(3)
Utah	136	114	127
Vermont	141	129	148
Virginia			
Total	3,510	3,621	3,287
White	904	875	783
Colored	2,606	2,746	2,504
Washington	415	397	334
West Virginia	(2)	1,399	1,381
Wisconsin	982	1,056	1,054
Wyoming	46	36	53
Total registration area[1]	42,208	40,388	40,467
White	22,966	24,119	23,774
Colored	19,242	16,269	16,693

As these figures are basic and official, and as they, with fuller figures later, will constitute the starting point for surveys of illegitimacy in this country for an indefinite time to come, it may be as well to describe in some detail how they are gathered.

It is only in recent years that the federal and State authorities have been sufficiently impressed with the importance of vital statistics to undertake a comprehensive compilation of them each year. Statistics of birth registration have been compiled, more or less carefully, by separate States for themselves for half a century or more, but it was not until about 1915 that the Federal Government undertook to establish on a systematic

---

[1] Exclusive of California and Massachusetts, the birth certificates of which States do not require information on illegitimacy.

[2] Not added to registration area until a later date.

[3] Not in registration area in 1925 and 1926.

basis the work of gathering them. Under the auspices of the Census Bureau, a "birth-registration area" was set up, covering those States only which could show an accuracy of at least 90 per cent in their birth returns. When the first annual report on births was issued by the Census Bureau, covering the year 1915, only eight States had met this requirement and been included in the area. But the additions since then have been comparatively rapid. For 1926, the latest year for which detailed returns are available, the area included thirty-five States and the District of Columbia, besides two other States which had been previously included, but were temporarily suspended. At the beginning of 1929 all the States in the Union were included except four, Texas, New Mexico, Nevada and South Dakota, and the first two of these were under test as to the accuracy of their figures. It will doubtless be but a short time until the whole country is fully covered.

In gathering the returns over this area, the Federal Government works through the States, but exercises as close a supervision as it can without having actual direct control. The primary reporting official is the local registrar. Each registrar in the country districts, as a rule, covers about as much territory as would be included in a single township, and in the cities as many registrars are appointed as the size of the place requires. Whenever a birth occurs it is the duty of the attending physician or midwife to fill in the birth certificate giving the pertinent facts and deliver it to the local registrar. This official is usually a physician, a physician's wife, a school teacher, or other person well acquainted in the community, who receives a small fee for each certificate, the fee as a rule being paid out of local taxes, collected under the authority of the State.

Under the most desirable practice the local registrar forwards the birth certificate direct to the proper State official, perhaps a director of vital statistics or an official of the State board of health. In some cases it is sent first to the county health officer, who sends it to the State official. The State authority makes what compilations he desires from the certificates received and then sends transcripts of them to the Census Bureau in Washington. Here the data from the millions of yearly certificates are compiled, and the figures are published in an annual report.

To insure the reasonable accuracy of these birth returns the Census Bureau is constantly carrying on tests in the various States of the registration area. Through its own agents and through questionnaires, it checks up on the births of a selected locality, and compares the results with the returns for that locality sent in from the State. In many cases these returns are found to be 100 per cent accurate. Rarely do they fall below the required 90 per cent line. But when they reveal a general looseness in the working of the system a State may be removed from the registration area until its returns again meet Federal approval. Only in two or three instances has it been necessary to take this step.

There is still, through the failure of local officials to make complete reports, considerable inaccuracy in the birth figures for the registration area, but they may be taken as representing a fairly close approximation to the actual facts. The same may be said for the illegitimacy figures, although they naturally include a still larger error factor than those for simply the number of births. There is always the temptation to record an illegitimate birth as legitimate in order to protect the mother and child. Published figures can therefore nearly always be regarded as too low. The degree of error can be judged from a number of intensive studies of special areas, figures for which will be given below.

In order to arrive at a tentative figure for the total annual illegitimate births in the United States we may take the figures in the above table as a basis and from them calculate the probable number in the country as a whole. On the basis of the 1920 census and the estimated rate of increase in the following years, the thirty-three States and the District of Columbia included in the 1926 registration area contained about 70 per cent of the country's population. The 40,467 illegitimate births for this area in 1926 would thus point to a total of about 58,000 for the whole country. But this is much too low. For the States outside the 1926 registration area contain a much larger proportion of negro population than those within it, and the illegitimacy rate is consequently much higher.

Within the registration area, on the basis of the 1920 population and the estimated increase since, there were in 1926 about 76,030,000 whites and 5,445,000 negroes, and outside this area 25,509,000 whites and 6,152,000 negroes. The recorded illegitimacy returns for the area in that year were 23,774 among the whites and 16,693 among the negroes, or an average of one birth to each 3,198 of the white population and one to each 328 of the negro population. These ratios would probably hold for the unregistered area also, and for the country as a whole. On this basis there would be, in 1926, approximately 33,000 illegitimate white births and 35,600 negro, or 68,600 all told. Since the projection of the registration-area ratio over the whole country on the basis merely of comparative population figures may not be considered sufficiently accurate, a closer estimate was sought by taking into account only the single, widowed and divorced women of child-bearing age, as revealed by the census returns. But this method resulted in practically the same figures, which may therefore be considered as approximately correct, so far as the actual returns made to the Government indicate.

Just how much these figures should be increased to cover births reported as legitimate, but actually illegitimate, it would be impossible to say. In nearly all instances where a careful study is made of the births in a given locality the reported number of illegitimate births is found to be too low. For example, Boston, in 1914, reported 752 live births as illegitimate, whereas an intensive investigation by the Federal Children's Bureau disclosed 95 others registered as legitimate, but really illegitimate. The reported number would thus have to be increased by about one-eighth. Similarly in Milwaukee the illegitimate births registered in 1916 were 420, and in 1917, 373. A survey showed 31 cases of live illegitimate births unregistered as such in 1916 and 37 in 1917. For the two years together the reported illegitimate births were thus nearly 9 per cent too low.

If this ratio of error should be applied to the white illegitimate births of the whole country the figure given above, 33,000, would have to be increased by some 10 per cent, and the total would stand at approximately 36,000. This is fairly close to other estimates made by investigators who have studied the subject closely.[1] However, it would be unsafe to assume on such slender grounds that the above ratio of error would hold good for the whole country, rural and urban alike, and it

---

[1] See "Illegitimacy as a Child-Welfare Problem," Part 1, by Emma O. Lundberg and Katharine F. Lenroot, published by the U. S. Children's Bureau, 1920.

would indeed be difficult to arrive at any ratio at all which would represent much more than a guess. We will probably be on safer ground to accept the statistical figure of 32,800 as a working basis, keeping always in mind that it is a minimum figure and in all likelihood considerably too low. It must be remembered also that the work of agencies organized to assist the unmarried mother, by its very nature, is concerned chiefly with those women and girls the fact of whose motherhood has become a matter of public knowledge. If the illegitimate birth is so concealed that it gets into the returns as legitimate the biggest part of the problem which the rescue homes attempt to solve has probably already disappeared.

ILLEGITIMACY AMONG NEGROES

Illegitimacy among negroes has been excluded from this study, not because there are no difficulties connected with it, but because it clearly constitutes a separate social problem. The extent of negro illegitimacy is hardly realized by the general public. According to the official Census Bureau figures, 12 per cent of the negro births in the registration area of 1924 were illegitimate, 11.7 per cent in 1925, and 11.8 per cent in 1926. In cities like Baltimore the percentage has been found to be as high as 24 per cent and in Washington, D. C., 19 per cent. Without discussing the causes of these high rates, it is sufficient to point out that they show clearly the wide difference in standards prevailing between the two races, and the lighter regard for the marriage ceremony which permeates negro communities. With such widespread acceptance of illegitimacy as almost a normal phenomenon, the social and economic handicaps connected with it largely vanish. The unmarried negro mother is not looked upon as an outcast, and does not particularly stand in need of the same sort of help as the unfortunate white girl who has violated the conventions of her race. While it would be easy to carry this conclusion too far, and while it would be cruelly unjust to assume that illegitimacy entails no sorrow or disgrace to negro girls in given cases, it yet remains obviously true that for the present the real field of work of protecting and reclaiming unfortunate women and girls lies with the white race.

AGE OF MOTHERS

In practical application of measures to assist the unmarried mother, it has been also found that the field is further delimited by another consideration, that of age. By far the larger part of cases of illegitimacy occur with girls between the ages of 15 and 21 or 22. Beyond that age the marriage rate rapidly increases, as does a knowledge of the world on the part of the women, and of how to take care of themselves. The following table shows the occurrence of illegitimacy by age groups among the white population of the registration area of the United States in 1926:

Age of Mother	*Number Illegitimate Births*
10 to 14 years	387
15 to 19 years	11,490
20 to 24 years	7,446
25 to 29 years	2,027
30 to 34 years	967
35 to 39 years	613
40 to 44 years	224
45 years and over	35
Unknown	585
Total	23,774

One-half the illegitimate births in this area (and the same proportion, no doubt, would hold good for the white race in the

[9]

rest of the country) thus involve girls who have not yet reached their twentieth year. If two more years should be included in this age-group the proportion would mount to the point where it would cover the great majority of all such births, and a still larger majority of those who need help. Certainly the three age groups, which include all girls and women below the age of 25, would cover nearly all the cases which would need the protecting care of social agencies.

To ascertain as definitely as possible how many illegitimate births occur over the whole country within the limits of these groups, we may assume that the ratio of the registration area holds good through the rest of the country and project that rate over the whole population. A more accurate method, however, would be to take into account only the unmarried women and girls within the specified age limits. Census figures for 1920 are available showing the number of women and girls in the age group 15 to 19 and 20 to 24. These were 4,183,000 for the two groups together, and using the official estimate of the rate of increase in six years they would number 4,634,000 in 1926. For the whole United States in 1926 the number of single, widowed, or divorced white women between 15 and 24 was 6,364,000. In the registration area 18,936 illegitimate births were recorded in which the mother's age came within this range, distributed among the 4,634,000 women. At this ratio, the number of such illegitimate births for the country as a whole would be 26,000, and adding the small number in which the mother was less than 15 years of age we have a total of 26,500 illegitimate births in the whole United States to white women of 24 years of age or less.

The comparatively low age of mothers of illegitimate children indicated by figures given above is attested also by other investigators. In a study made in 1921, Dr. George B. Mangold, University of Missouri, presents the following table comparing the ages of such mothers in selected regions:

LOCALITY	DATE	NO. CASES	AGES	
			Percentage under 21	Percentage 21 and over
Washington, D. C.				
White	1913	113	37.17	62.83
Colored	1913	487	65.5	34.5
Philadelphia				
White	1915	591	52.9	47.1
Colored	1915	364	65.9	34.1
St. Louis				
White	1912-13	1,079	55.7	44.3
Colored	1912-13	271	69.7	30.3
Australia	1910-12	20,691	37.05	62.95
Ohio	1913	1,290	60.1	39.9
Baden, Germany	1902	4,284	31.8	68.2
U. S. birth registration area	1918	22,765	45.2[1]	54.8[1]

Commenting on these figures, Dr. Mangold says: "Surprising differences seem to exist in regard to the proportion in each age group. In Baden it is low among those under 21; in the American cities it is higher, while in St. Louis and in Ohio the number is excessively large. In fact, more detailed figures indicate that illegitimacy among American girls of 15, 16 and 17 is far more common than among German girls, and these facts hold for both colored and white girls. In the American cities it appears that a greater incidence of illegitimacy occurs among girls in the eighteenth and nineteenth year of their lives than at any other period. At 18 girls become marriageable and beyond this age the proportion of single girls rapidly declines. Accordingly the higher age groups offer less relative opportunity for illegitimacy. In Baden, however, the twentieth year represents the age of greatest frequency, and the leading years are 19 to 23, inclusive.

---

[1] Age classification for birth-registration area "under 20" and "20 and over."

"In Germany a much larger proportion than in the American cities are more than 25 years of age. The births in Berlin may, for the purpose of illustration, be compared with the white births in St. Louis. In the former city, 32.3 per cent of the unmarried mothers were over 25; in the latter city only 15.9 per cent. On the whole, it appears that immorality manifests itself in the early years of life of the young woman in America and rather quickly runs its course. In Germany it appears later and lasts longer. As a consequence a large proportion of American girls are immature and with difficulty able to care for their babies, while in Germany the great majority are mature in years if not in mind."

Residence in Urban and Rural Districts

In addition to considerations of color and age, a third feature of the problem which has in the past tended to narrow the field of effective operation of institutions for the unmarried mother is the occurrence of illegitimacy in the more remote country districts, where a temporary escape for the unfortunate girl is practically out of the question. The most advantageous location for such institutions is a quiet and secluded suburb of a large city, and most of them are so located. They thus draw upon the population of the city and surrounding regions, both rural and urban, and extend their help also to girls from farther removed country districts who are able to break away from home. With the very rapid opening up of the country through the medium of the motor car and of good roads, the possible field of activities of rescue missions, maternity homes, and like institutions is naturally increasing and will continue to increase as such traffic grows. But naturally there will always remain a considerable number of unfortunate girls who, because of poverty or other handicaps, are unable to come to the city for help.

Such girls can not, of course, be statistically classified. But some idea of their number may be obtained by noting the number of illegitimate births in rural districts as contrasted with those in cities and towns, as it is reasonably safe to assume that most such country births represent cases where the mother would have traveled to a city far removed from her own community if she had been able to do so. (That, of course, applies only to white girls. There appears to be very little removal of colored girls to the city because of imminent illegitimate childbirth.) The following table, compiled by the Census Bureau, shows the number of illegitimate births in country and city districts in 1926 in each State included in the registration area:

STATE	Total[1]	White Native	Foreign	COLORED
Arizona	109	70	36	33
Urban	49	33	13	5
Rural	60	37	23	28
Connecticut	355	302	52	62
Urban	245	203	42	56
Rural	110	99	10	6
Delaware	68	66	2	138
Urban	24	23	1	42
Rural	44	43	1	96
District of Columbia	120	70	5	438
Urban	120	70	5	438
Florida	333	324	7	1,065
Urban	176	169	6	271
Rural	157	155	1	794
Idaho	95	90	3	—
Urban	38	35	2	—
Rural	57	55	1	—
Illinois	1,679	1,454	159	382
Urban	1,136	943	140	341
Rural	543	511	19	41
Indiana	706	695	10	150
Urban	356	347	8	126
Rural	350	348	2	24
Iowa	617	600	12	28
Urban	426	410	12	21

THE CARE OF THE UNMARRIED MOTHER

State	White			Colored
	Total[1]	Native	Foreign	
Rural	191	190	—	7
Kansas	400	387	9	84
Urban	220	213	3	68
Rural	180	174	6	16
Kentucky	709	708	—	438
Urban	137	136	—	176
Rural	572	572	—	262
Maine	373	336	33	—
Urban	120	102	17	—
Rural	253	234	16	—
Maryland	491	472	18	1,308
Urban	280	265	14	736
Rural	211	207	4	572
Michigan	1,595	1,394	193	189
Urban	1,267	1,086	175	172
Rural	328	308	18	17
Minnesota	960	905	48	46
Urban	647	611	32	12
Rural	313	294	16	34
Mississippi	240	237	1	3,437
Urban	36	36	—	306
Rural	204	201	1	3,131
Montana	122	104	14	13
Urban	76	63	11	—
Rural	46	41	3	13
Nebraska	457	430	22	37
Urban	252	237	13	16
Rural	205	193	9	21
New Hampshire	114	102	12	1
Urban	52	44	8	—
Rural	62	58	4	1
New Jersey	637	541	95	366
Urban	416	343	72	267
Rural	221	198	23	99
New York	2,458	2,025	427	433
Urban	1,972	1,577	391	388
Rural	486	448	36	45
North Carolina	1,111	1,068	2	3,821
Urban	266	252	1	708
Rural	845	816	1	3,113
North Dakota	259	244	15	9
Urban	115	108	7	—
Rural	144	136	8	9
Ohio	1,896	1,775	110	456
Urban	1,262	1,160	94	401
Rural	634	615	16	55
Oregon	199	187	11	7
Urban	160	151	8	2
Rural	39	36	3	5
Pennsylvania	3,882	3,636	233	93†
Urban	1,883	1,711	166	821

STATE	White Total[1]	White Native	White Foreign	COLORED
Rural	1,999	1,925	67	110
Rhode Island	205	167	34	21
Urban	192	156	32	19
Rural	13	11	2	2
Utah	126	116	9	1
Urban	63	57	5	—
Rural	63	59	4	1
Vermont	148	132	13	—
Urban	59	52	4	—
Rural	89	80	9	—
Virginia	783	774	6	2,504
Urban	173	171	1	768
Rural	610	603	5	1,736
Washington	312	264	41	22
Urban	262	221	36	8
Rural	50	43	5	14
West Virginia	1,157	1,149	6	224
Urban	200	196	2	54
Rural	957	953	4	170
Wisconsin	1,015	948	54	39
Urban	602	559	35	9
Rural	413	389	19	30
Wyoming	43	37	5	10
Urban	14	13	1	1
Rural	29	24	4	9
Total	23,774	21,809	1.697	16,693
Urban	13,296	11,753	1,357	6,232
Rural	10,478	10,056	340	10,461

[1] Including cases in which country of mother was not stated.

OCCUPATION

An important factor in the consideration of the assistance that can be rendered the unmarried mother in the United States is the occupation of the mothers previous to the birth of their babies. From a study of some 10,000 cases in the principal cities of the United States during the years from 1924 to 1928, the writer has prepared the following table:

PERCENTAGE OF UNMARRIED MOTHERS IN SPECIFIC OCCUPATIONS

	Washington	Philadelphia	Cleveland	N. Y. City	Milwaukee	Boston	Detroit
Domestic or House-keeper	41	54	42	42	39	51	40
Factory worker	20	21	27	22	32	33	27
Office	9	3	10	9	5	3	9
Clerk	7	3	4	11	13	5	11
Student	12	10	7	4	4	3	9
Miscel-laneous	11	9	10	12	7	5	4
Total	100	100	100	100	100	100	100

A comparison of these figures with those given by Dr. George B. Mangold [1] would indicate that in the past 10 to 15 years there has been a large decrease in the percentages of mothers employed as domestics and a corresponding increase in those employed in factories. This probably reflects the smaller percentage of all women now employed as domestics as compared with earlier years. Another noticeable change is the large increase in the number of school girls. The average percentage for six cities in Dr. Mangold's study was about 2½ per cent, while in the later statistics for seven cities the percentage had increased to 6.

The relation of domestic service to illegitimacy has been commented upon by a number of investigators of juvenile delinquency and its relation to employment. It is most probable that domestics as a group are somewhat below the average in education and have lower moral standards. Other causes mentioned are the loneliness of life, the lack of opportunities for making friends and securing recreation and amusement in safe surroundings, and the monotonous and uninteresting character of the work. The same factors are largely responsible for the

[1] "Children Born Out of Wedlock," page 68.

considerable percentage of unmarried mothers recruited from factory workers. Borosini [1] states that "most unmarried mothers are recruited from among poorly paid and insufficiently protected industrial workers and domestics."

EDUCATION

The educational history of unmarried mothers in the United States seems to be fairly typical of that of the mass of the people. The writer has examined the records of some 10,000 cases in the principal cities of the United States for the years 1924 to 1928, from which the following table has been prepared:

SCHOOLING RECEIVED BY UNMARRIED MOTHERS

(Percentages)

	Washington	Philadelphia	Cleveland	New York	Boston [2]	Milwaukee	Detroit
Under 8th grade	55	57	58	70	65	60	62
8th grade	33	36	35	25	28	33	32
High School	12	7	7	5	7	7	6
	100	100	100	100	100	100	100

[1] "Problems of Illegitimacy in Europe."
[2] C. R. Preston, executive secretary of the Florence Crittenton League of Compassion, Boston, states that 50 per cent of the girls in that home in the years 1924-28 had High School Education. This home as well as all Florence Crittenton Homes receive a much better class of girls than the average.

CHAPTER TWO

PRIMARY CAUSATIVE FACTORS IN THE PREGNANCY OF UNMARRIED WOMEN

There are two methods of approach to the study of causes leading up to sex acts on the part of unmarried women which result in the bringing into the world of children born out of wedlock. Both of these have been used extensively by authorities and in recent years they have been combined, notably by Dr. Percy Gamble Kammerer in his book, "The Unmarried Mother." All of the earlier studies seem to have been based on the environmental history of the woman in question, using as material case records secured from various agencies dealing with unmarried mothers and delinquent girls and women. The accuracy of the conclusions reached by this method, not taking into account the failure to give due emphasis to the mental aspect of the individual under study, may be challenged upon several grounds. Among these may be stated (a) the limited number of records available to the student, and (b) the inaccuracy of the records, due, first, to misstatements on the part of the woman to shield her family and friends and often the man in question, as well as to hide her own true attitude towards life in general, and, second, to the fact that the records were generally made by inexperienced and untrained persons with no definite plan in view when they were being compiled.

The second method of approach has been through a study of adolescence, and its relations to sex problems. Since the writings of Havelock Ellis, Kraft-Ebbing, Moll, Forel, Forester,

Hall, Freud and Jung, students have realized that mental conflicts manifested at early periods of childhood are precedents of sexual misconduct in many girls and young women which may lead to pregnancy. Modern research has brought to light the fact that the sex instinct begins to develop in children within a very short period after their birth. Havelock Ellis maintains that autoerotic manifestations may sometimes be observed in infants of less than twelve months. Stanley Hall, Moll, and S. Freud point out many instances showing sexual life in children even as young as 5, 3, or even 2 years, and Freud has described a boy of 5 years whose chief interest centered in sex.

In any consideration of infantile sexualism and its effect upon children in later years, the views of S. Freud and the school of psycho-analysts must be given careful consideration. Stanley Hall, after summing up the Freudian conceptions of sex, holds that if they are accepted it follows that not only must sex pedagogy begin in the cradle, but that it is of prime necessity for the education of the feeling, will, and intellect, and that sex in its larger sense contains the promise and potency of life. From the first moment of birth, Nature begins to prepare the infant for future parenthood. In view of the above, Dr. Kammerer points out that the infantile state of the child is clearly one in which particular care must be taken in order that sex instincts may not be submitted to traumatic experiences. Excessive coddling, pettings, and strokings should be avoided as far as possible, as they may become precedents of later undesirable behavior on the part of the child. Dr. Kammerer has made an interesting analysis of the Freudian theory, especially in its relation to the unmarried mother. He says that only recently have students come to recognize what a tremendous portion of energy is absorbed in the solution of the sex question during childhood. Children oscillate for months between the acceptance of fairy tales and the impressions which drift into their consciousness from without, and so severe is the strain of this reconciliation that some of them become neurotic. It is at this time that the shock attendant upon the realization of the true sex processes, coming suddenly into a consciousness that is wholly unprepared for its reception, causes unfortunate results. Especially to girls does the method of reproduction appear to be nauseating, monstrous, and cruel, creating an attitude of mind in which not only the parents, who have submitted to this degrading experience, seem lowered, but the whole question of sex as well. Weak, nervous systems can obviously be injured by a shock of this kind.

By the time of school days children accumulate a considerable amount of misinformation on sex matters, which slowly gives place to knowledge. An incredible amount of meditation goes on within this field. Stanley Hall draws attention to the fact that we adults forget this because we have submerged its traces. Here again psycho-analysis penetrates into the earliest strata of psychic evolution and brings the material to light as the basis of many perversions. Many sex aberrations are now being explained by their genesis, as due to arrest or magnification in early life. It is during this ferment that innocent young maidens spin reveries full of flaring absurdities and contradictions, and the whole horizon of consciousness is filled, now by one theory, now by another. On top of this mental unrest begins the psychological impulse, normally produced, of a state of tension, and the individual sways between resolution and impulse, between restraint and the desire for gratification. It is just here, says Stanley Hall, that the strain lies.

[21]

THE CARE OF THE UNMARRIED MOTHER

With keen psychological insight and in a charming and vivid manner, Stanley Hall in his treatment of adolescent development pictures the inmost thoughts of a young girl of 12, listless, unresponsive, self-centered; brooding over great biological questions, the origin of life, sex, death, her own relation to her parents and brothers; musing about marriage, about how to get at the truth, both to escape and to penetrate the mesh of conventional lies of every sort, culminating with those of sex, with which she is encompassed. Girls then are quite unaware of what physical and mental changes are taking place within them. "How shall they know the truth, what they most of all want to learn?" he asks, "and how can they go on without asking and being put to shame, or without seeming ignorant, when, in fact, perhaps all assume that they do know? They ought and perhaps do sometimes blush in secret to think of these things, but they can not escape the insistent questionings. How can their elders be so blithe and cheery if the world is as they are beginning to divine it? How they muse on certain incidental words or allusions let fall by the grown-ups, which answer perhaps some of their mute longings, while all the rest of the wiser talk washes over them unnoted and leaving no trace! These frequent suggestions are pondered in the heart; and thus the girl slowly orients her way to wisdom by them, constantly casting old knowledge, once thought precious, as rubbish to the void. She will reach the goal in the end; but how vastly much might have been saved her by a little plain, sane teaching betimes! And how this long stage, which is throughout so vulnerable to shock, might have been shortened and facilitated! Whether they are saved to virtue or lost to vice often depends upon their getting or failing to get the knowledge their whole souls are consciously or unconsciously seeking."

Peculiarities of family organization which create person-ality problems of compensation in children have an important part in their sex development. Dr. E. T. Krueger [1] sums this phase as follows:

1. Lack of affection in childhood and adolescence, in situa-tion of over-strict control through severity, austerity, cruelty, patriarchal aloofness, or through the prevention of normal ro-mantic contacts, thus frequently making the child either unfit for sex life by emotional deficiency, or by placing a premium upon affection when encountered later. The normal family as a "unit of interacting personalities" operates to develop emo-tional attitudes in the child. The father, for example, makes the girl emotionally dependent upon a man, and the mother makes a boy emotionally dependent upon a woman, thus pre-paring the child for adult love of the opposite sex.

2. Over-affection on the part of the parents, creating abnor-mal emotional needs, easily stimulated. When separation from the parents occurs, or when incorporation into the wider social world in adolescence or adult life takes place, response contacts may be found to be overpowering.

Dr. Krueger, in the same paper, cities two other reasons that may be classified as mental rather than environmental causes:

1. The meagerness of interests and values not associated with sex which normally operate to prolong the adolescent years and to divert attention from sex. Education promotes such values; so do recreation and religion. Their absence per-mits sex to become an early interest among the masses who lack the incentives of intellectual and social pursuits, and lead to child marriages, and not infrequently to sex relations outside of marriage.

---

[1] "Problems of Adolescence," F. C. Conference, Nashville, Tenn., May 2, 1926.

2. The prevalence of the idea that romantic love is the chief source of happiness. We have developed in modern life the cult of love to such an extent that romantic love is made the goal of existence and colors all adolescent relationship between the sexes. The idea of romantic love, coupled with the much freer sex mores of today, is probably one cause operating toward illicit sex relations. To be sure, new rituals have developed to control romantic contacts, but romantic love in one social organization or one economic and cultural class may lack the social rituals and realizations which another class builds about it.

Methods Used in This Study. While due consideration has been given by the writer to the factors of mental characteristics which explain sex abnormality, greater stress has been laid upon environmental history, as the data available are more readily analyzed and become more understandable to the average person interested in the problem of the unmarried mother. Furthermore, the present trend in behavior analysis is away from a biological and toward a sociological explanation. Just a few years ago we were saying that the problems of adolescence were chiefly concerned with sex maturation. Irregular sex behavior was rather constantly defined as some pathology of the biological process of sex. We heard much also of an innate raging sex appetite or instinct, common to all persons, which was likely to get out of hand and land a youth in a moral jam. Now, as a matter of fact, we are seeing comparatively few cases of sex misconduct which we can define as cases of biological sex abnormality, and we are discovering that adolescents do not necessarily go about with terrible passions. No attempt has been made to classify or put into statistical form the data gathered from the material available to the writer, first, because of the extreme difficulty of tabulating the varied and complex human emotions and situations that enter into the problem, and, secondly, because the overlapping of causes makes it difficult to ascribe to any particular one the definite reason for sex irregularity. The writer, however, has placed in sequence the causes of delinquency, according to his conclusions as to their relative importance.

Low Standards of Behavior. No person who has dealt with girls who have had irregular sex experiences that bring them to the attention of private or public agencies, can fail to be impressed with the fact that the great majority come from families or early childhood situations which have failed to transmit social definitions of behavior, and to fix attitudes which are in conformity with the culture of organized society. Broken homes, helpless and incompetent mothers, drunken fathers, overburdened parents, and poverty prevent the effective organization of the family and child. From an early age the child lives in an atmosphere where obscenities prevail, excessive drinking is customary, incest not uncommon, and vice and loose morals may be actually encouraged. It is also found that habituation in childhood to ideas of sex irregularity, so that emotional attitudes of repugnance or disapproval are not transmitted to the child, is not uncommon. It is from this class of girls, with low standards of behavior, that the ranks of the prostitutes are largely recruited.

The process generally begins with sex initiation of the child at an early age. Gradually her delinquency increases until she becomes so involved that her misdoings are brought to the attention of the authorities. Continued delinquency makes it necessary that she be committed to an institution where she remains for a period of years. Upon her discharge, she is either hardened by her experiences and joins the ranks of the prostitutes, or, having received a new viewpoint of life and higher standards, often successfully marries and takes a normal place in society.

The reformation of girls with low standards of behavior presents problems of great difficulty. The substitution of high standards for low standards is a long and tedious process. It is often far easier to raise the standards of the child than to raise the standards of parents. For that reason, where family or early childhood situations are such as almost to defy remedy, authorities have deemed it wise to remove the child from such situations.

Bad Home Conditions. Bad home conditions is one of the major causes of illegal sex relations which often result in unmarried motherhood. It is a factor so closely connected with that of low standards of behavior that it is almost impossible to separate them, as bad home conditions are generally the principal cause of low standards of behavior. But there are differences that cause the writer to place the last-named as a more important factor in delinquency. When bad home conditions are remedied or improved, or the girl is removed to a more wholesome atmosphere, the lack of decent standards of conduct may bring her to a moral downfall. Furthermore, it is found that many girls escape pregnancy, although subject to demoralizing conditions within their own homes, because of their underlying moral vitality.

In his study of 500 cases of unmarried mothers, Dr. Kammerer gives bad home conditions as a major factor in 194 cases, and as a minor factor in 158 cases, or as a factor of some degree in 352 cases. These results closely approximate those secured in his study of more than 10,000 cases by the writer, who believes that low standards of conduct, coupled with bad home conditions, are responsible for approximately one-half of the cases of unmarried motherhood in the United States.

The circumstances responsible for bad home conditions are so well known to all social workers that it is not necessary to enter into a discussion of them. It might be well, however, to mention a few of the principal influences that produce delinquency.

Lack of Parental Control. By reason of death of one of the parents, separation, or divorce, illness of the mother or father or other causes, the life of the young daughter is not properly supervised or controlled during the formative period. She is allowed to come and go at will, to make undesirable acquaintances, to visit questionable places of amusement, and generally to live a life free from all restrain.

Parents—Alcoholic, Immoral, or Criminalistic. The habits of parents, such as alcoholism on the part of either or both parents, produces results varying from indecent language to actual sex assault, and from poverty at home to a lack of physical stamina in the children due to undernourishment. Immorality on the part of the mother so warps the judgment of the daughter in regard to sex ethics as to make her an easy victim of her own impulses. Criminalistic habits on the part of either parent break down all moral standards, and delinquencies of various kinds are observed in their children.

Poverty. Poverty, while not a factor at all in the cause of pregnancy among unmarried women, operates by intensifying the bad conditions already existing in the home. As Dr. Kammerer points out, from the point of physical development, for instance, one can appreciate that undernourishment may easily weaken a young woman's power of resistance to sex temptation, and one can understand how the lack of spending money operates as a factor, preventing wholesome recreation and normal social life, and so making these girls too dependent on men for their enjoyment.

Overcrowding. Overcrowding, often caused by the taking of boarders, breaks down a girl's feeling of privacy, and so brings on a loss of self-respect and modesty. It is frequently necessary for several persons to share the same room, and often three or more to occupy the same bed. Incest sometimes follows. Married couples sleep in the same room with their children, and as a result the latter are initiated at an early age into the intimacies of married life.

Quarreling, Abuse and Other Irritating Conditions. Unhappiness at home, caused by quarreling, abuse, nagging on the part of relatives, etc., often produces a spirit of such unhappiness to girls that they are driven into excesses of various kinds, or leave home for new lodgings where they may be exposed to new temptations. Very often this factor is introduced by the action of parents in taking from their daughters all their earnings for the support of the family.

Bad Environment. Closely associated with the factor of bad home conditions is that of bad environment. But there is a difference that requires a separation of the two. Very often a girl is compelled to live away from home in a lodging house which is detrimental to her well-being. Then again her place of employment often produces contaminating conditions. Bad environment is particularly dangerous to the immigrant girl who comes alone to find a home in a new land, and to the country or small-town girl who goes alone to a large city to find employment. The former, separated from all the family ties to which she has been accustomed, often feels that to be an American she must adopt without question many of the false standards which she sees about her; the latter often feels that in order to be up-to-date she must follow the practices of the experienced city girl. Lodging houses are often located in the vicinity of vicious neighborhoods, and the young girl who is compelled to live in such surroundings finds that vice is constantly before her eyes. Scenes of debauchery, drunkenness, and prostitution become so common that they are soon accepted as matters of course.

Conditions of employment are a factor of considerable importance, and the girl who is employed in places where she is brought in contact with men of low morals is in a far more dangerous situation than the girl more advantageously employed. Waitresses in restaurants, manicurists in barber shops, chambermaids in hotels, are constantly confronted with many temptations.

Low Mentality. Low mentality is one of the major causes of illegitimacy. It is represented in various degrees, from the feeble-minded girl, totally incapable of distinguishing between right and wrong, to the girl with some mental peculiarity which makes her particularly susceptible to suggestions of sex delinquency.

Estimates of the proportion of mental defectives among unmarried mothers in the United States vary so widely that it is almost impossible to approximate their number. One worker at the National Council of Charities and Correction in 1915 seriously announced that her investigations showed that 98 per cent of the unmarried mothers with whom she had come in contact were feeble-minded. It is the opinion of the writer, after consultation with many officials of agencies dealing with unmarried mothers, that perhaps 10 per cent of the girls who enter rescue homes are definitely feeble-minded, and that perhaps another 10 per cent are border-line cases. According to the consensus of these officials, and contrary to popular opinion, the mentally abnormal girl is not necessarily possessed of extraordinarily developed sex instincts, but rather of marked undeveloped inhibitions.

Dr. Kammerer, reaching the same conclusion, after careful examination of all the factors that enter into mental abnormality and its relation to illegitimacy, observes that while a feeble-minded girl is in constant danger of becoming pregnant, emphasis should be laid on the fact that her pregnancy results not so much from abnormal sex desire as from an inherent incapacity to adjust herself to the life of the community.

The care of the feeble-minded girl is one that deserves most careful consideration. Every girl of this class should receive care in institutions, especially for the feeble-minded, during the child-bearing period, exception being made in those cases in which absolutely adequate supervision can be provided by relatives and friends. It is a great mistake to send her to training schools for delinquents, as she can not be benefited by her stay in the institution, and her presence often raises difficulties in the training, leading to the reform of normal individuals. Nor should the feeble-minded unmarried mother be admitted to maternity homes, established for the rehabilitation of unfortunate girls. There is no cure for the mental defective and but slight improvement will be shown even under the most favorable circumstances.

Officials of rescue homes are more concerned with the treatment of border-line cases than they are with the low-grade, feeble-minded girls. The latter can be sent to a State institution for permanent custodial care, but the former present problems that are difficult to handle. Very often girls of the border-line type are attractive in appearance and possess special capacity along certain lines. Mentally, however, they are still children and always will be. Their sex impulses are governed by the age of physical maturity. Their powers of inhibition and their mental comprehension depend upon such control as can be exercised by a mind of ten or twelve; by a child mind incapable of realizing the necessity of our accepted moral and social standards. Weak minds and weak wills, clothed in mature and attractive bodies, therefore, succumb to the tempter or deceiver, and before long the young woman may herself ensnare her male acquaintanceship. Sex impulse, when the control thereof has been lost to a person (man or woman) of weak will is almost unconquerable. It leads the young girl into the juvenile court, and sends her to a reformatory. It drives the older girl into prostitution, or imposes upon her the burden of unlawful motherhood. It also makes seduction and betrayal easier, because the woman can not summon the mental power to protect herself.[1]

---

[1] Consult "Children Born Out of Wedlock," by Dr. George B. Mangold.

CHAPTER THREE

MINOR CAUSATIVE FACTORS IN THE PREGNANCY OF UNMARRIED WOMEN

In addition to the primary factors discussed in the previous chapter, there are certain contributory factors as well as certain major factors beyond the control of the girl in question. The contributory factors include bad companions, unwholesome recreation facilities, educational disadvantages, desire for experiences, and alcoholism. The other main factors include assault, rape, and incest. To the latter might be added betrayal after promise of marriage. Dr. Kammerer, in addition to all of these, finds that children born out of wedlock often come to women with abnormal sexualism.

Bad Companions. Bad companions generally follow the primary factors of bad home conditions and bad environment, but not always. Often a girl who has a happy home located in a desirable neighborhood is thrown with companions in school or at work or through improper recreation, who have a detrimental effect upon her character. Many instances of sexual delinquency are found where a girl begins her career at the suggestion and instigation of those with whom she associates. For instance, two couples, one of the girls already promiscuous, start on a picnic or holiday. The girl who has been initiated into sex irregularity may put the other into a position where a false standard of sportsmanship may prove her downfall.

Unwholesome Recreation. Bad environment, improper home conditions, monotony of life on farms and in small towns, make it difficult for a girl reared in these surroundings to enjoy normal recreational advantages. Hence for her pleasure she is forced to take part in forms of recreation that are not only demoralizing by their very character, but throw her into contact with persons of doubtful moral standards. In the cities these unwholesome recreations include those supplied by public dance halls, unsupervised and unchaperoned, largely patronized by men for the sole purpose of meeting attractive girls and persuading them to surrender their virtue; excursions on lake and river steamers, where staterooms are often easily obtainable for immoral purposes; cabarets and night clubs where liquor is either sold or pocket flasks of intoxicants are passed from drinker to drinker; amusement parks, with their highly intensified and exciting recreations; moving-picture theaters, especially those where "midnight" shows attract an undesirable element; and burlesque and cheap vaudeville theaters where extremely suggestive performances are the rule.

In the country the greatest danger lies in road houses and places where barn dances are held. These places have been greatly developed since the automobile has made transportation comparatively simple.

Perhaps no other form of recreation is producing more cases of irregular sex relations today than "joy" rides in automobiles. This refers both to the country and the city girl, as it makes it possible for either to move in social worlds to which they are not accustomed, and provides a means by which the individual, if he so desires, can escape the moral world in which he might otherwise be constrained. It should be pointed out, however, that the automobile permits the members of social groups, geographically distributed, to maintain connections and thus enables families and other groups to preserve personal contacts. As a means of wholesome recreation it has no equal, offering as it does a means for the city girl to go to the country and get in touch with Nature and its wonders, and for the country girl an opportunity to enjoy the sane amusements of urban life. But unfortunately in the hands of unprincipled men the automobile becomes an agent of extreme danger. The simple ride into the country or to town often turns out to be a journey of several hundred miles. Stops are made at road houses or questionable resorts, or along deserted roads where "petting," often innocently commenced, ends in ruined lives. The convenience of an enclosed automobile, virtually a room on wheels, makes illicit sexual relations easy. Breakdowns, accidental or intentional, prolong the return to the early hours of the morning. Fear of parental displeasure at the late arrival inclines the girl to accede to the request of her male companion to go away with him. Even a ride after dinner on a summer night is fraught with danger, especially if the man is of strong, wilful character, and the girl is weak, sentimental, affectionate, and has no very strong standards of behavior. Often a few drinks of illicit liquor from a pocket flask give the added touch that brings about the moral relaxation and surrender of will power that spells disaster.

The payment on the part of the girl for recreational favors from men deserves mention. Young women are made to understand that they are receiving pleasures and enjoyment which can be paid for adequately in only one way.

Educational Disadvantages. This factor must be considered in two phases. First, the failure of parents and teachers to give girls, especially in the adolescent period, some interest in life that will keep them from brooding over questions of sex, and, second, the failure to instruct children on sex matters. The importance of the first has long been realized by psychologists. The absence of healthy mental interests produces a type of vacant-minded dreamer who most readily succumbs to temptation, and who possesses no capacity for substituting absorbing mental interests for preoccupation with the affairs of sex.

The second phase is often found as a factor in the cases of young girls who claim that pregnancy was the result of lack of instruction on sex matters. There is no doubt that a large number of girls are actually woefully ignorant of the nature and expression of the most dominant instincts of life.

Desire for Experiences. Within the past eight or ten years an increasing number of girls have given as a reason for their pregnancy the desire to experience sex relations. The number, while yet small compared with the total of illegal pregnancies, is still large enough to show the trend of the times. It is surprising that such cases do not occur more often when one considers the wide publicity that is given to sex irregularities, the flood of magazines and novels that deal with the erotic side of sex, and the public discussions by prominent men and women of the right of youth to live its own life.

Alcoholism. While the use of intoxicants is sometimes given by girls as a reason for their pregnancy, it is found to be a factor in such few cases as to be relatively unimportant. It is sometimes an important contributory cause, because it weakens the powers of inhibition and makes its victims susceptible to suggestions of many kinds. Drinking on the part of young girls, which has largely increased within the past ten years, tends to inflame their emotions and weaken their will power to such an extent that they readily yield to the importunities of their male companions.

Assault, Incest, and Rape. Several hundred girls in the United States become mothers every year because of conditions beyond their control. They are victims of assault, rape, or incest. In practically all instances these cases occur in families where the home conditions or environments are bad.

Betrayal After Promise of Marriage. The number of girls who claim that they were betrayed after promise of marriage is comparatively small. There is a natural desire on the part of a girl, when first interviewed, to throw the blame for her behavior on the man, and the result has been that many surprising attempts to concoct stories that would succeed in this endeavor have been found. But there are many cases in which the girl has really been deceived by men who have promised marriage. In some instances deliberate deception has been practiced, and in others the man may have honestly intended at first to marry the girl, but was delayed for financial or family reasons until his ardor cooled.

Sexual Suggestibility. Dr. Kammerer, in his study of the causes of illegitimacy, devotes three chapters to a discussion of abnormal sexualism, sexual suggestibility in general, and sexual suggestibility by one individual. He finds the second of these a major factor in 26 and a minor factor in 16 out of the 500 cases which he examined, and the third a major factor in 38 cases and a minor factor in 4 cases. The writer has not found any of these causes such an important factor in the cases which he has studied. There is, of course, the oversexed girl to be found in every rescue home, but few of them will admit that they have been brought there by a raging sex appetite which they could not control.

CHAPTER FOUR

ORGANIZED AGENCIES TO ASSIST THE UNMARRIED MOTHER AND HER CHILD

From the statistics of illegitimacy published in Chapter One of this study, it is apparent that there are approximately 36,000 cases of illegitimacy among white women in the United States annually. This number has been practically stationary for several years, and because of the wider sex education of girls, the improvement of economic conditions, and the more widespread knowledge of contraceptive measures, it is not expected to increase. Approximately one-fourth of this number live in rural districts far removed from remedial agencies, and up to the present time their problem has not come to the immediate attention of social agencies. For many years to come the only practical help that can be given them is through rural nurses in their own homes. Another large percentage consist of women who are living in some loose form of relationship with the father of their child or children, and their problem does not greatly differ from that of the legal mother living under practically the same economic conditions. Still another considerable percentage of the illegitimate births occur in the families of well-to-do people who handle the problem entirely as a family matter. The girls, often under assumed names, are delivered of their babies in private maternity hospitals and arrangements are made privately for the adoption of the child or for its future care in some other manner. These cases rarely come to the attention of social agencies.

There remain some 19,000 to 20,000 cases annually of illegitimate births in the United States that present problems to public or private agencies. In practically all of these cases assistance must be rendered the unmarried mother during confinement, and plans made for the future of the mother and child. It is safe to say that fully three-fourths of this number require hospital facilities for confinement. Statistics of large cities show that nearly 80 per cent of all illegitimate births occur in hospitals or maternity homes. In Michigan, out of 1,617 illegitimate children born in 1925, 1,038 births took place in hospitals or maternity homes.

PUBLIC AGENCIES

The public agencies, entirely supported out of public funds and not including criminal and juvenile divisions of city and county courts, that deal with the unmarried mother and her child consist of State Welfare Boards and Children's Bureaus, State institutions for delinquent girls with maternity departments, State institutions for feeble-minded girls, State maternity homes, State hospitals (generally connected with State medical colleges), county supervisors or commissioners, county welfare boards, county almshouses and hospitals, and municipal hospitals and city authorities.

State Aid to Unmarried Mothers and Their Children. Within recent years and especially since the passage of the act by the United States Congress for the promotion of the welfare and hygiene of maternity and infancy, known as the Sheppard-Towner Act, every State in the Union has increased its program for the aid of mothers and their children, and in consequence the unmarried mother finds that in many places she can turn to the State for assistance. Few States have gone so far as Minnesota, which outlines its responsibility in its illegitimacy statute as follows: "To safeguard the interests of illegitimate children and to secure for them the next possible approach to care, support, and education that they would be entitled to if born in lawful marriage." Definite responsibility is placed upon the State in the following provision of its 1917 law:

It shall be the duty of the Board of Control when notified of a woman who is delivered of an illegitimate child, or pregnant with child likely to be illegitimate when born, to take care that the interests of the child are safeguarded, that appropriate steps are taken to establish his paternity, and that there is secured for him the nearest possible approximation to the care, support and education that he would be entitled to if born of lawful marriage. For the better accomplishment of these purposes the Board may initiate such legal or other action as is deemed necessary; may make such provision for the care, maintenance, and education of the child as the best interests of the child may from time to time require, and may offer its aid and protection in such ways as are found wise and expedient to the unmarried woman approaching motherhood.

Every State has established a department which deals with problems of maternity and infancy. These are designated in various ways, such as State Board of Control, State Board of Health, Department of Public Welfare, State Board of Charities, etc. Under practically every one of these boards is a Children's Bureau, which is primarily interested in the child, and usually no distinction is made between the legitimate child and the one born out of wedlock.

The assistance given to the unmarried mother by these agencies is the same given to all mothers and generally follows certain definite programs.

(a) Establishment of permanent prenatal and child-health centers and provision of a permanent source of information on maternal and infant care.

(b) Child-health conferences, which have a twofold purpose—that of disseminating information on the care and hygiene of infants and preschool children, and that of examining so-called well children and pointing out to the parents any deviations from the normal that are found.

(c) County health units which provide home visits to mothers, infants, and preschool children, prenatal and child-health conferences, classes for mothers, girls, and midwives in which maternal and child care are taught, and super-vision of midwives.

(d) Home visits made by itinerant nurses, paid in full or in part from maternity and infancy funds, by which mothers are taught the importance of prenatal care and its influence on their own well-being and on that of the unborn infant, the importance of breast feeding, and the hygiene and care of infants and preschool children.

(e) Classes for adults and girls ("Little Mothers") where instruction is given by nurses in the care of the baby and the preschool child, bathing, dressing, and feeding the baby, regulation of its habits, methods of preparing formulas, diet, and the prevention of communicable diseas s.

(f) Inspection of maternity homes and boarding homes of babies.

(g) Distribution of literature, lectures, etc.

State Institutions for Delinquent Girls. Every State has an institution for delinquent girls and many of these have maternity departments which care for pregnant girls committed by the courts. Grounds for commitment differ in the various States. In one State 90 per cent of the commitments were because of sex delinquency. In another State the following nature of offenses may be taken as typical:

Against the person	2
Larceny	21
Stubborn, delinquent, wayward	70
Sex offences	64
Other	27
Total	184

When it is found that the girl is pregnant her confinement takes place either in the maternity department of the institution or in a public hospital, and upon the birth of the baby she is returned to the institution and her baby placed with relatives or adopted, or she is paroled to return home with her baby. In practically all institutions of this kind breast feeding is insisted upon, and an effort is made to have the mother keep her baby. Practically all of the State institutions for delinquent girls do some sort of follow-up work, and in addition the girl and her child are kept under supervision of probation officers.

State Institutions for Feeble-Minded Girls. A comparatively small number of illegitimate children are born to feeble-minded mothers committed to State institutions because few institutions of this kind admit pregnant women. Practically none have facilities for maternity work and in the few instances that occur the accouchement takes place in a public hospital. The child becomes a ward of the State and is usually cared for in a State institution for children. After the birth of the baby the feeble-minded mother is returned to the institution to which she is committed.

State Maternity Homes. Massachusetts and Nebraska have State institutions for the confinement and care of women both married and unmarried from all over the State. In Massachusetts the State Infirmary is located at Tewksbury. Expectant mothers from the State institutions for delinquents and mental defectives are also sent here for maternity care. In 1927 there were 105 births at the Infirmary, of which 95 were illegitimate. Before discharge from the Infirmary a protective plan is made for the mother and child. Relatives are communicated with, positions in domestic service secured, or other plans made. Each case is investigated from the point of view of legal action to secure support from the father. In the after-care work the cooperation of private societies and of individuals is sought.

Advice, counsel, and supervision are given, and every attempt is made to reestablish the mother in her community and to enable her to keep her child. In Nebraska the State institution is located at Milford, and is called the Nebraska Industrial Home. It had an average number of 92 inmates during 1927, and 113 babies were born there in that year.

State Hospitals. Many States support, entirely or in part, general hospitals in connection with the medical colleges connected with their State universities. There are 26 hospitals of this kind in operation. Confinement care is supplied free to all mothers who can not pay for it and no distinction is made between the legal mother and the unmarried mother. The mother remains in the hospital for a period of two weeks to a month. Practically no follow-up work is done by these institutions, but in nearly all instances mothers and babies, needing care, are brought to the attention of county or State welfare boards or private agencies.

State Pensions for Mothers. Some 43 States have adopted mothers' pension laws, which make it possible in some instances for unmarried mothers to keep their babies. Two of these, Michigan and Nebraska, specifically make provision for "unmarried mothers," while one State, Wisconsin, provides for a "mother without a husband." In Indiana, Maine, Massachusetts, New Hampshire, North Dakota, and Washington, where the law applies to any mother with dependent child or children, and in Colorado, where it is made applicable to "any parent or parents," it would seem possible to extend the benefits of such laws to the mother of an illegitimate child; yet these States impose such restrictions as to character as may be interpreted to preclude such mothers. In 29 States the benefits of the law extend only to mothers of children born in wedlock. In this connection it might be added that the Federal act providing for allotments, allowances, and compensation to dependents of soldiers and sailors includes children born out of wedlock among the beneficiaries if support has been ordered by the court or if the child has been acknowledged by the father.

County Aid to Unmarried Mothers. Under the political organization of practically all States the county is the unit which is primarily responsible for the needy unmarried mother who is a resident of that county. County welfare boards, county commissioners, and supervisors of the poor are generally charged with the responsibility of extending aid to all persons in distress. Forms of assistance include care in almshouses or county hospitals, visits by county nurses, and allowance from the county funds. In cities where the legal organization is separate from that of the counties similar aid is extended by the city authorities.

County Almshouses. The number of births of illegitimate children that take place in county almshouses is decreasing, due to a more enlightened attitude toward the unmarried mother, yet it is sufficiently large to cause comment. In some sections of the country, especially in the South, the almshouse is the only refuge for the unmarried mother at the time of her confinement.

County and Municipal Hospitals. In practically every community of several thousand inhabitants in the United States there is a public hospital, supported entirely by public funds, or a hospital with which the city or county has a contract to take care of the indigent sick. In practically all of these institutions there is no limitation as to nationality, religion, color, age, or condition of health. Expectant mothers, both married and un-married, who are without any financial resources, enter the hospital a few hours, or at most a few days, prior to the date of the confinement and are discharged as soon as they are strong enough to be on their feet. Nearly all of the hospitals of this kind have a social service department that makes an effort to put the unmarried mother and her child in touch with social agencies.

PRIVATE PHILANTHROPIC AGENCIES

The private philanthropic agencies are divided into two classes:

(a) Agencies doing general family case work.
(b) Agencies doing a specialized piece of work, such as maternity homes, hospitals, child-caring agencies, etc.

General Agencies. In practically every city in the United States there are organized bodies for doing charitable work to which the unmarried mother can turn for assistance in her time of need. Such bodies in many places are known as the Associated Charities. In other places they bear more distinctive titles. For instance, in New York City are found such organizations as the Association for Improving the Condition of the Poor, the Charity Organization Society, the Maternal Aid Society, the Salvation Army, the Volunteers of America, etc. In addition to these agencies that help all needy persons, irrespective of color or religion, there are certain denominational relief societies to which the unmarried mothers who belong to a particular religious denomination turn. Thus, in many cities are found such organizations as the Catholic Charities, United Hebrew Charities, Mission of Help (Protestant Episcopal), etc.

Specialized Agencies. First among the specialized agencies are the maternity homes, organized for the specific purpose of dealing with the unmarried mother and her child. Maternity homes generally fall into one of three categories:

1. Temporary homes that receive unmarried mothers prior to or after their confinement and give them shelter for a short period of time until they can be transferred to another institution, returned to their homes, or otherwise disposed of.

2. Maternity homes that keep the unmarried mother for a considerable period of time, provide for prenatal and postnatal medical care for the mother, and care for the child.

3. Maternity homes that have complete hospital facilities and give the patient prenatal, confinement, and postnatal care, and care for the child.

In both of the last two, provision is generally made for domestic or vocational training while the mother is in the home, and follow-up work after she leaves.

There are approximately 225 maternity homes of the three classes located in the United States. (For list see Appendix.) During 1928 these institutions cared for approximately 12,000 white unmarried mothers and 9,000 illegitimate children. Allowing for a certain amount of duplication due to the rendering of assistance to the same girl by one or more homes, it is safe to say that one-half of the white unmarried mothers who required assistance during the year in question passed through the hands of these agencies.

Florence Crittenton Homes. Approximately one-third of the maternity homes in the United States bear the name of Florence Crittenton, and are affiliated in an organization known as the National Florence Crittenton Mission, whose headquarters are located in Alexandria, Virginia. There are now 65 Florence Crittenton Homes located in 38 States. In 1927 these homes cared for 5,359 girls and 3,005 babies. They had assets valued at $4,631,000.

The first of these institutions was established by Charles N. Crittenton, a wealthy New York druggist, in New York City in 1883, in memory of his daughter Florence, who died at the age of four years. After establishing the first home Mr. Crittenton gave himself unreservedly to this work, and in the course of the next 25 years (until his death in 1909) established similar homes throughout the United States and in foreign countries. During his lifetime he gave more than $500,000 for the purchase of property, and in maintaining the institutions, and at his death left about $250,000 to the national organization which was established to carry on his work. In 1896 he became associated with Dr. Kate Waller Barrett of Atlanta, Ga., wife of the Rev. Robert S. Barrett, Dean of St. Luke Cathedral in that city. Dr. Barrett had become interested in the work for the unmarried mother nearly 20 years earlier, and had established in Atlanta one of the first maternity homes in the South. In 1898 the homes which had been established by Mr. Crittenton as independent units formed a national organization under the name of the National Florence Crittenton Mission. In the same year a charter was granted to this organization by the United States Congress, and it was the first national organization for charitable and philanthropic work to be so chartered by Congress. In 1903 the charter was amended by Congress, and it is under this revised charter that the National now operates. Dr. Barrett succeeded Mr. Crittenton as President, and upon her death in 1925 she was succeeded by her son, Robert S. Barrett.

In the beginning the Florence Crittenton Homes were principally rescue homes for the temporary care of unfortunate girls and women who wanted an opportunity to give up their immoral lives. Great stress was laid on appealing to the religious side of their natures and this emphasis is still an important part of the work of the organization. While the management is Christian and Protestant, it admits girls of all religious faiths, and no influence is used to make them change their faiths. The establishment of maternity wards has been greatly extended, until now nearly all of the Crittenton Homes have well-equipped maternity wards that provide prenatal, confinement, and postnatal care. In those where there are no such facilities the girls are sent to private or public hospitals for their accouchement. The work of the Florence Crittenton Homes at the present time is devoted almost entirely to the care of unmarried mothers and their babies, and especial effort is directed to the girl of high school age who has made her first mistake.

Each home is a separate entity, governed by a local board which makes its own rules and regulations, according to conditions in the territory which it serves. Three principles, laid down by the founder and adopted by the National Florence Crittenton Mission, are generally observed:

1. The mother must be kept in the home for a sufficient time so that she may be brought into contact with the higher and better things of life, prepared for the responsibilities of motherhood, and trained to care for her baby and for her own future.

2. Motherhood is often the means of regeneration; hence the mother must be kept with the child for the influence it will have upon her.

3. The child needs the maternal care that only a mother can give; hence it should not be separated from the mother except when it is clearly shown that both for the mother's sake and that of the child it is desirable.

Insufficient financial support, lack of accommodations, differences of opinion among social workers, ignorance of the social problem by physicians and trained nurses, apathy on the part of the board members, over-emphasis on the part of those interested in the welfare of the child, and incompetent supervision, have made it impossible to establish firmly these three principles and to adopt uniform rules that will put them in practice in every Florence Crittenton Home, but on the whole they are generally in force.

Girls enter the homes from two to four months prior to the time of their confinement, and remain from three to six months after the birth of their baby. A majority of the homes require the girls to remain for six months after their confinement. Breast feeding is insisted upon. During their stay in the homes the girls are given educational and religious instruction, taught to care for their babies, and trained in domestic science. Special courses of instruction are given to those preparing for commercial or secretarial positions or those who expect to take up nursing as a profession.

While the girls are in the home plans are made for their future. In practically all cases they provide for the keeping of mother and child together, and adoption is not agreed to except as a last resort. Keeping track of the girls who have left the home has always been an important part of the work, and this feature has been greatly improved in recent years by the employment of experienced social workers.

The Florence Crittenton Homes are supported by interest on endowments, voluntary contributions, and entrance fees of the girls who are able to pay. The average fee is $50 for the time the girl is in the home.

Salvation Army Homes. The Salvation Army has 34 homes and hospitals for unmarried mothers located throughout the United States. In practically all of these well-equipped hospitals provide for prenatal, confinement, and postnatal care. The maternity work is under the immediate direction of the Commander of the United States forces, Miss Evangeline C. Booth, and the National Secretary, Colonel W. F. Jenkins, whose headquarters are in New York City. For the purpose of administration, the country is divided into four territories, viz.: Eastern, Southern, Central, and Western, and each of these divisions is in the charge of an officer of the Army. On January 1, 1929, the officers in charge were as follows: Eastern Territory, Lieut. Col. Clara Van de Schouw, 853 Broadway, New York City; Central Territory, Lieut. Col. Annie J. Cowden, 713 N. State Street, Chicago, Ill.; Western Territory, Brigadier Sophia Harris, 115 Valencia Street, San Francisco, Calif.; and Southern Territory, Col. Martha Hamon, 54 Ellis Street, Atlanta, Ga.

The Salvation Army has four training schools for officers, and, while these schools are not wholly devoted to the training of officers for work with unmarried mothers, in the case of any student (cadet) who is likely to be assigned to that work special instruction is given. After ten months training in the training school, each officer, when assigned to her particular field, puts in a year of probationary service at the hospital or maternity home to which she may be appointed. Periodical conferences of officers interested in this particular work are held at which problems relating to the work are discussed.

The Salvation Army receives all unmarried mothers irrespective of age, color, or religion. Two of their homes are solely for colored girls. The girls are received from two to three months prior to their confinement and remain for an average of three months after the births of their babies. While in the home they are trained for their future, and are given educational and religious instruction. Following up the girls after they leave the home and assisting them in every way possible is an important part of the Army's work.

Denominational Homes. A number of the homes for unmarried mothers in the United States are under the auspices of some denominational church, and, while they generally care for girls irrespective of their religious affiliation, it is natural that most of the inmates or their families are members of the particular church which is interested in the home. The Roman Catholic Church has the largest number of these institutions, and they are located in the principal cities of the United States. These institutions should not be confused with those which bear the name of the House of the Good Shepherd. The latter are exclusively for delinquent and wayward girls, generally from 12 to 16 years old, or girls who have been committed by the court or by their families for a definite period. Expectant mothers are not admitted to these institutions. The Protestant Episcopal Church has 12 homes for girls which are known as Houses of Mercy. They are located in the eastern and central parts of the United States.

Hospitals Operated on a Philanthropic Basis. General and maternity hospitals under private management, largely supported by voluntary contributions from the public, care for a large percentage of the unmarried mothers in the United States annually. The rules of admission, the charges for treatment, and the character of service rendered the mother and her baby after they leave the hospital, vary widely according to the institution. In Philadelphia, for instance, there were, in 1921, 26 hospitals of this type offering maternity care to mothers out of wedlock, out of which 19 gave this service free. Four accepted white patients only and two colored only. Nineteen made no restrictions as to race. Eleven hospitals admitted women in their first pregnancy only (three of these admitting emergency cases of later pregnancy). In practically all of these hospitals some attempt was made to do social service work, or the aid of an outside agency was enlisted.

Commercial Maternity Homes. There are several hundred commercial maternity homes in the United States, most of which are small institutions operated by physicians or trained nurses and having accommodations for from two to ten mothers. The number has decreased greatly in recent years, owing to the restrictions placed upon this type of institution by the various States and the requirement that they be licensed and regularly inspected, and that they make full reports to the State. Commercial agencies are not particularly concerned with the moral rehabilitation of the mother, and they usually intimate to the applicant that they will dispose of the child. In fact, in many cases, they urge the woman to give up her child at once, so that the way may be opened for the erring one to return to her friends and family without suffering disgrace and ostracism.

Usually the cost to a girl entering a commercial maternity home is as high as the traffic will bear. The advertising matter sent out generally announces very reasonable charges—from $5 to $10 per week for room and board and from $25 to $50 for confinement. But once in the hands of one of these homes the girl is practically helpless and must accede so far as possible to the wishes of the person in charge. In case her family or friends have means, extras of one kind or another are added until the bill reaches large proportions. Instances have been known where bills of more than $1,000 were rendered for extra surgical work and fear of exposure compelled its payment.

The wholesale adoption of babies and the profits resulting therefrom have been somewhat diminished in recent years because of the more stringent regulations of the States regarding adoption, but still much is done clandestinely. Both the mother and the agency desire the least publicity possible, and as little connection with legal machinery as is necessary. Therefore they often fail to file adoption papers, and if anything is done at all, it must depend on the demand of the foster parent. Frequently he is too ignorant to understand the importance of his act, or he connives in the failure to make out a deed of adoption, thus relieving himself of full responsibility for the child later should the acceptance of such responsibility prove burdensome or undesirable. That a heavy mortality occurs among these babies is practically inevitable. An instance is cited by Dr. Mangold of an investigator in St. Louis who inquired at one of these homes for a baby and was urged to take the baby away with her, although the institution knew nothing about the social and moral status of either the investigator or her "friend." In Chicago, in reply to a question, "What shall we bring to get the baby?" referring to evidences of one's eligibility for the care of an adopted baby, the simple reply was, "Oh, bring a shawl."

CHAPTER FIVE

LEGAL PROTECTION FOR THE UNMARRIED MOTHER AND HER CHILD

All too often do social agencies fail to appreciate the full importance of taking advantage of the legal resources open to them in their work of helping the unmarried mother. In many cases they are not familiar with the extent of the protection afforded by the laws. But usually it is the expectant mother herself or her family who shrink at the mention of legal action. Recourse to the courts is nearly always held to entail the one development they most want to avoid—publicity. In spite of a natural sympathy with this feeling, agency workers will be well advised, as a rule, to stress the value of taking whatever help the law holds out, pointing out the future importance to the child of having its paternity fixed, and to both mother and child of having financial help. The mother will often be willing enough to accept this help, once she realizes her rights under the law.

Without minimizing the value in particular instances of such matters as giving the child its father's name, legitimation for inheritance purposes, etc., it may be taken as assured that in the great majority of cases with which agencies have to deal the greatest benefit to be derived from legal action will come from the two objectives named, (1) the fixing of the child's paternity through court adjudication, and (2) the placing of at least a part of the financial burden of rearing and educating the child where it properly belongs, namely, on the father's shoulders.

In the great majority of cases even the far-too-small amounts usually granted by a court help out materially in securing proper care for the child. In the absence of other help, it may mean the difference between life and death for the infant. In any event a regular weekly or monthly payment probably will be worth more during these first years than at any other time of life. The unmarried mother who has formed an attachment for her offspring will be easily led to appreciate these facts and induced to apply to the courts for the aid to which she is entitled.

The extent to which she can secure this aid has been broadening in recent years, and the value of court action correspondingly increased. It will be highly desirable for every agency to formulate for itself a definite plan of legal procedure. This will naturally vary with the locality. But it must be based on the course which such cases take in the courts, and this course is much the same everywhere. The several steps usually comprise: The filing of a formal complaint before a justice; the issuance of a warrant by the justice for the accused man; the holding of a preliminary hearing from which the justice determines whether a *prima facie* case has been made out; the holding of a formal trial, and if the verdict favors the plaintiff the rendering of a judgment; enforcement of a judgment, through causing the father to pay a single specified amount or to contribute periodically to the child's support, perhaps in the charge of a probation officer.

While all the workers in a home will find a knowledge of these legal matters useful, it is highly advisable that one particular member of the agency staff, or an outside worker, shall act as contact official, keeping in touch with available and competent legal talent and standing ready to bring the unmarried mother or expectant mother in touch with the legal machinery of the region. In the nature of the case the most effective worker for this service, other things being equal, will be the one in charge of the follow-up work of the home, so that a check can be had on the continuance of financial support from the father, once it has been ordered by the court. In many cases legal advice can be had from a friendly lawyer on the board of the home. In others such help can be obtained from lawyers showing a general interest in local charities through the assistance of local boards of charities. Some cities have bureaus which afford free legal advice to the poor, and these may be utilized without hesitation.

When the question arises as to what precise rights the law may give to mother and child and what is the proper method of procedure to obtain them, no general answer can be given. Laws of the forty-eight States differ widely. Workers of a given agency, however, can soon familiarize themselves with the provisions in their own State, and after following through a few actual cases can come to a good working knowledge of the most advisable procedure. When situations arise involving action in other States, however, it must be remembered that each case is to be considered on its own merits, as the procedure in dealing with one State may be quite different from that in dealing with another.

It is only in comparatively recent years that much attention has been given to advanced illegitimacy legislation by the various States. Under the British common law, which became the American common law, the illegitimate child was regarded as "nobody's child," and his civil status, particularly with regard to such matters as the inheritance of property, was and is based upon that idea. British statutes, however, dating back to the time of Elizabeth, have charged the father as well as the mother with responsibility for the child's support, and this subject of support has been the chief feature of illegitimacy laws enacted by our States. Led by Virginia in 1785, some States have also adopted measures looking towards a more favorable civil status for the illegitimate child; but until the last fifteen or twenty years there can not be said to have been any very active interest in the subject among legislative bodies. The three modifications of the common law which have been adopted by most States were those enacted by Virginia at the start, namely, provision for legitimation by subsequent marriage, and provision for legitimating the issu of certain annulled marriages, and provision for natural inheritance between the illegitimate child and its mother.

The awakened interest in the subject in recent years has led to the passing of much legislation, all tending in the direction of a more humanitarian attitude toward both mother and child. In 1917 Minnesota passed a law which is often referred to as a model illegitimacy law. North Dakota in the same year went so far as to declare every child the legitimate child of its father as well as its mother—the only State to assume this radical position. The desirability of working toward some standard practice among the various States has long been felt, but it was not until after the World War that much progress in this direction was made. Since 1915 the Federal Children's Bureau has interested itself in illegitimacy problems. In 1920 it called two regional conferences, in New York and Chicago, to discuss the subject of legislative standards and if possible to agree upon a set of recommendations. As one outcome of these conferences a "syllabus of propositions to serve as basis of a program for illegitimacy legislation" was drawn up and approved.[1] As another an appeal was made by the Children's Bureau to the National Conference of Commissioners on Uniform State Laws to draft a proposed act or acts for the protection of illegitimate children. Such an act was drafted by a committee, presented to the 1921 meeting of the Conference, discussed and modified, and finally adopted in 1922. This is the Uniform Illegitimacy Act, which for the present forms the most definite legislative objective of social workers and others interested in promoting the welfare of illegitimate children and their mothers.

The Uniform Illegitimacy Act has been adopted, in principle, by five States, North Dakota, South Dakota, New Mexico, and Arizona in 1923 and Iowa in 1925. In a number of others, particularly in New York, it has influenced legislation. Its sponsors did not expect or desire that every State should incorporate it bodily into the State's code of laws, recognizing that previous practices, differences in public opinion, etc., make a certain diversity inevitable. But "agreement with respect to certain basic principles," says the Children's Bureau, "is essential. Especially with reference to status and property rights and jurisdiction is such general agreement needed." As a matter of fact most of the recommended provisions are already in force, to a greater or less degree, in the various States.

As it stands now the Uniform Illegitimacy Act concerns itself with but one of the two chief divisions of the subject of illegitimacy law. These two divisions are (1) the "status"

---

[1] See "Standards of Legal Protection for Children Born Out of Wedlock," U. S. Children's Bureau Publication No. 77, page 20.

laws, defining the position of the illegitimate child in the community and involving such matters as legitimation, inheritance between the child and its mother and father, etc., and (2) the "support" laws, providing for the maintenance of the child and care of the mother during the birth period. The Uniform Act covers only "support" measures. The first draft of the proposed act covered both divisions. But unexpected and vigorous opposition developed to the proposals which looked toward placing the illegitimate child on the same legal level as the legitimate, and it was thought advisable to abandon these provisions. The proposed act accordingly is simply a "support" act, having as its chief objective the insuring of an adequate share in the financial burden on the part of the father. In brief, its provisions are as follows:

1. As a basic principle the act asserts that the parents of an illegitimate child owe it the necessary maintenance, education, and support. This, says Prof. Freund, chairman of the committee which framed the act, is an innovation, as no such obligation is laid by the common law, and no general statement of the father's duty in this relation is included in American statutes. Among the practical consequences to which it leads is the possible recovery from the father or his estate of expenditures on the child. Another feature not covered by present laws is that the liability for payment of such expenditures extends to the father's estate as well as to the living father.

2. The main body of the act deals with statutory provisions to enforce the "support" obligations of the father. These cover the bringing of the complaint, preliminary hearings, the trial, the judgment if the complaint is found justified, and the enforcement of the judgment. For the most part they follow

present legislative practices. Complaints are made by the mother, or if the child is or is likely to be a public charge, by the authorities charged with its support. A complaint may be made to any judge or magistrate having power to commit for trial. If the preliminary hearing shows probable cause the defendant is required to give bond for his appearance at the next term of the proper court, and in default of bond may be put in jail.

The trial shall be by jury if either party so requests. If the verdict is against the defendant the court gives judgment against him, declaring paternity and for the support of the child. The judgment is to be for annual amounts until the child is sixteen. The judgment may also provide for the payment of the necessary expenses incurred at the birth of the child.

Payments may be made either to the mother or to a trustee. The defendant must give bond for these payments, in default of which he may be put in jail or at the court's discretion committed to the custody of a probation officer. If he gives bond and defaults on any payment the bond shall be forfeited, and he may be put in jail for contempt of court.

An important provision of the act is that any compromise made with the father for support of the child is binding only when adequate provision is fully secured by payment or otherwise, and when the arrangement is approved by the court. The court has continuing jurisdiction over "support" proceedings until the judgment is fully satisfied and also continuing jurisdiction over the custody of the child.

3. Failure to support the child by the father who has acknowledged paternity or whose paternity has been adjudged, and failure to carry out a judgment for such support, are made misdemeanors.

4. Notable provisions regarding jurisdiction are included. Proceedings to compel support may be brought either in a court of the State where the mother or child resides, or is found, or in that of a State where the alleged father is a permanent or temporary resident. It is not a bar to the jurisdiction of the court that the complaining mother or child lives in another State. A judgment for support rendered in another State may be made valid, through proper court action, for the State in which the Uniform Act is adopted.

The Uniform Act is thus not proposed as an ideal illegitimacy act so much as one which offers improvements over most of those now in force in the various States and which presumably stands a good chance of being adopted in principle. Within its scope it would beyond doubt work a great improvement in the care of both mother and child if adopted by all the States. As noted, however, it incorporates provisions already widely prevalent. It will be interesting to glance at the variations of the laws of the different States with respect to the chief points covered by the proposed Uniform Act.[1]

Support Provisions.

Who May Make Complaint. Five States, Missouri, New Mexico, Texas, Virginia, and Washington, have no legislation at all providing for support of illegitimate children. In most of the rest the expectant or actual mother may make complaint and in many States the local poor-relief official may also do so under specified circumstances. This corresponds closely with the provisions of the Uniform Act.

---

[1] As given in Children's Bureau Publication No. 42, "Illegitimacy Laws of the United States, Analysis and Index," by Prof. Ernst Freund.

While the general intent is much the same in the laws of nearly all the States there are slight differences in the wording of the statutes which may on occasion take on some importance. In the following States "any single woman" may make complaint: Alabama, Colorado, Florida, Mississippi, North Dakota, Ohio, and Tennessee. In North Dakota the county commissioners also have this right and in Mississippi the board of supervisors in cases where the child is likely to become a public charge. In Ohio, if an unmarried mother fails to bring a charge, the proper officers of town or county interested in the support of the child, or the director of the county infirmary, if the mother becomes a charge therein, may file complaint. Tennessee provides that a justice may, on his knowledge, cause an unmarried mother to be brought before him after the birth of the child.

The longest list of States is made up of those whose statutes give the right of complaint to "any woman pregnant with or delivered of an illegitimate child," although this exact phrasing may not always be followed. They include: Arkansas, Connecticut, Delaware, Illinois, Indiana, Kansas, Maine, Michigan, Minnesota, Montana, Nebraska, New Hampshire, North Carolina, Oregon, South Dakota, Utah, Vermont, Wisconsin, and Wyoming. In many of these States the laws also contain supplementary provisions for bringing the illegitimacy case into court. In Connecticut, if the mother does not bring a complaint and the town is not indemnified for its expenditures, the town officials shall bring proceedings. In Delaware any justice on his own knowledge or information that a woman has had an illegitimate child shall cause her to come before him and discover the father, or give bonds to indemnify the trustees of the poor. On her failure to do either he shall commit her to jail. In Michigan the right of complaint lodges with the superintendent of the poor of the county where the mother asks aid.

Minnesota's law provides that the county board of the county where the mother resides, or any member of it or of the State board of control may apply to a justice or a municipal court to inquire into the circumstances. Many other States in the above list take similar precautions to help them shift expenses to the shoulders of the father when the mother fails to bring an action on her own account. Nebraska gives the right of complaint to the county commissioners, and New Hampshire to the same officials or to the town selectmen. North Carolina county commissioners may act (if the mother is single) on an affidavit that the child may become a public charge, and in Oregon, under such circumstances, any public official may cause the mother to be brought before a justice after which a warrant may be issued. Vermont gives her overseers of the poor this privilege of bringing the mother before a justice, and they may prosecute in her name. Wisconsin county or town officers and Wyoming county commissioners have the right of making complaint.

Other States have varying but in general similar provisions of law. In the following States the right of complaint rests with the persons or officials names:

New York: Any woman, or a poor officer.

California: The mother or guardian.

District of Columbia: The mother, board of charities, or next friend.

Georgia: The justice on his own knowledge or on information under oath where the child may become a public charge.

Iowa: Any person may make complaint, which must be in

writing and must state that an illegitimate child has been or is about to be born and must accuse father.

Kentucky: An unmarried woman delivered of a child.

Maryland: Any justice on information that a woman has an illegitimate child shall cause her to be brought before him and to indemnify county for any charge unless she discloses the name of the father.

Massachusetts: The State Department of Public Welfare shall prosecute all cases if mother has no settlement in the commonwealth.

New Jersey: Overseers of the poor of a township, or if child is an inmate of a public institution an officer of that institution, may complain, the action in the latter case being for relief of the institution.

Oklahoma: Any person may make complaint. County commissioners required to bring proceedings if child or mother likely to become public charge.

South Carolina: Any woman delivered of an illegitimate child.

Rhode Island: Overseers of poor may make complaint. Where a single woman pregnant with or delivered of a child has no residence in the State, the agent of State charities has all powers and duties of the overseers of the poor.

West Virginia: A single woman, or a married woman living apart from her husband for one year, delivered of a child may make complaint.

Time of Complaint and Time of Trial. In most States complaints may be made either before or after birth, the list of those which specifically so provide including the following: Arizona, Arkansas, Colorado, Connecticut, Delaware, District of Columbia, Florida, Georgia, Illinois, Indiana, Iowa, Kansas, Maine, Maryland, Mississippi, Michigan, Minnesota, Massachusetts, Montana, Nebraska, New Hampshre, New Jersey, New York, North Carolina, North Dakota, Ohio, Oklahoma, Rhode Island, South Dakota, Tennessee, Utah, Vermont, Wisconsin, and Wyoming.

In several States the trial must come after birth, the following having provision of law to that effect: Arkansas, Delaware, Illinois, Maine, Maryland, Michigan, Minnesota, Mississippi, Nebraska, Rhode Island, South Dakota, and Utah. This is in line with the provision of the Uniform Act, which requires that trial shall be held after birth unless the person charged with being the father consents to have it held before birth.

Several States set a time limit after which no proceedings can be instituted. In Alabama complaint is barred after one year from birth of child unless the accused has in the meantime acknowledged or supported the child. In Colorado proceedings must be within one year after birth, in Illinois, Indiana, Kansas, and the District of Columbia within two years, in Connecticut and Kentucky three years. Maryland has a two-year limit unless some payment has been made by the accused.

Massachusetts provides that proceedings may be started immediately after the child is begotten, and the trial may be held before the child's birth unless the defendant objects; if he objects, there can be no action taken until the mother is advanced six months in pregnancy. Mississippi requires that a mother's complaint shall be made within a year after the child's birth, and a complaint by supervisors within a year after the child has become a public charge, but not after it is ten years old. New Hampshire officials may make complaint only within a year after birth, and the same limit applies in North Dakota, although the time in which the father is not an inhabitant of the State or not usually residing in it is not counted in the year.

If he deems proper, a justice in North Carolina may postpone trial until after birth, but action must be taken within three years. South Carolina requires that both complaint and trial shall come after birth. In West Virginia also proceedings may be instituted only after birth, with a time limit of three years. Utah has the longest time limit, four years, not counting the time in which the accused is absent from the State.

Process and Trial. Actions brought under illegitimacy statutes are classed as civil cases, but they have a quasi-criminal character. The Uniform Act follows the tradition for such legislation in providing that, after complaint has been made, "the judge or magistrate shall issue his warrant for the apprehension of the defendant, directed to any officer in the State authorized to execute warrants, and such warrant may be executed in any part of the State." It further provides, however, that with the consent of the complainant, "a summons may be issued in the first instance as in other civil cases, instead of a warrant, which summons shall be personally served." The latter provision marks an advance over present laws prevailing in practically all States, the warrant being the instrument used throughout the country to bring the accused to court.

The procedure with respect to a preliminary hearing recommended in the Uniform Act conforms to the practically universal present practice. It involves a hearing before a justice, at which the defendant has the right to be present, and upon showing of probable cause a binding over of the defendant, with sufficient security, to the proper court, the defendant being

committed to jail in default of such bond. The chief difference in existing practice among the several States lies in the
extent to which the justice goes into the merits of the case at the
preliminary hearing. In West Virginia the justice merely
examines complainant under oath and reduces her statement to
writing, binding the defendant over with no further inquiry.
The rule in most States, however, is that defendant shall have
the right to cross-examine the complainant, and the latter must
show probable cause. In Arizona and one or two other States
the accused may avoid further court action by making specified
payments at the preliminary hearing. In New Jersey the
mother may be compelled to disclose the name of the father,
failure to do so being contempt of court, and in North Dakota
she must give the name of the father and tir. e and place of
conception. Only in two or three States is there specific provision that the public may be excluded from the preliminary
hearing on request of either party.

The trial itself proceeds in most respects like that of any
other civil case. In nearly all States trial by jury is either
specified or made subject to the request of either party,
although in a few instances, as Tennessee, for example, jury
trial is obtained only when the case is appealed. In a number
of States provision is made for carrying on the trial even in the
defendant's absence. There is a general absence of provisions
for excluding the public from these trials, Michigan being one
exception. In Minnesota, however, all records of court proceedings in illegitimacy cases are withheld from inspection and
no copies are furnished to any except parties in interest or upon
orders of the court.

Judgment. When the verdict of judge or jury is against the defendant and no appeal is taken the question of the proper judgment arises. Practically always this is left to the discretion of the court, with such limitations as the law may prescribe. As the case is a civil one judgment takes the form of requiring payment of a given amount by the defendant as a contribution to the future welfare of the illegitimate child rather than as damages or punishment.

Beyond question payments made in illegitimacy settlements, in and out of court, have in the past been lamentably inadequate. A sort of tradition has grown up to the effect that such payments shall be small—a tradition accepted too often by courts as well as public. But with growing recognition of the moral and legal responsibility of the father for at least the partial support of the child the tendency toward increasing the amounts demanded of him has been growing strongly in recent years.

Of equal importance to the amount of the father's financial contribution to the maintenance of his child is the manner in which it is made, whether in a single lump sum or in periodical payments. There are good arguments favoring both plans. The chief contention of those who advocate lump-sum payments is that a smaller amount in hand is worth a much larger total whose full rendering is uncertain. As a typical example we may take the results of an investigation made several years ago in Milwaukee County, Wisconsin. In a given period, 86 fathers were ordered to make periodic or lump-sum payments of specified amounts for the support of their illegitimate children, or entered into agreement to do so approved by the district attorney. Of these, 47 were required to make, or agreed to make, periodic payments until the child was 16 years of age. Four of them, however, elected to make a lump-sum payment, as permitted by the statute. Of the 86 fathers, therefore, one-half were to pay periodically and one-half in lump-sum totals.

At the time when the period of investigation closed, the aggregate of the periodical payments should have been $14,961.50. The amount actually paid, however, was $6,307, or only 42 per cent of the required amount. The average amount ordered or agreed upon for each child during the 21 months' period in question was $318, or $15 per month; the average amount paid was only $134, or $6.38 per month.

The lump-sum payments required or agreed upon aggregated $13,820, or an average of $321.39 for each child. The amount actually paid was $13,675, or an averaᵍe for each child of $318. At the usual rate of disbursement this amount would cover only about 3 years and 4 months of the child's age.

Although many like instances could be cited the trend of opinion among social workers and other students of illegitimacy problems is strongly in favor of the periodical payment. The lump-sum payment is nearly always too low. It is likely to be quickly dissipated, leaving the problem of support still unsolved. As the primary object is the maintenance, education, and care of the child, for which the father should be held at least jointly responsible, his responsibility should be a continuing one so as to insure, as far as possible, the accomplishment of the object of the payments.

These ideas are reflected in the provisions of the Uniform Act which provide for the payment of specified annual amounts, equal or varying in the discretion of the court, in support of the child until it is sixteen. In this respect it is fairly in line with much of the existing legislaton. Usually the judgment rendered consists primarily of an order for support, which in large measure is left up to the court to define in each individual case, taking into account the peculiar circumstances of that case. For the most part judgments are for periodical payments, the amounts, within limits, being left to the discretion of the judge. In some cases, as in Colorado, the jury sets the amount. In Connecticut, the father shares with the mother the cost of maintaining the child as well as the cost of confinement. In Delaware, the defendant is required to pay $10 for confinement expense, $10 to the attending physician, and not less than $5 nor more than $25 to the mother or the custodian of the child. Florida sets a maximum of $50 per year, as the required contribution to the support, maintenance, and education of the child, and the same provision holds in Alabama. In Kentucky the jury decides how much is payable per year and how many years it is to be paid, and the judge specifies the frequency of payments. Maryland puts the maximum monthly payment at $15, while certain other States, as California and Maine, simply require that the father shall help maintain and educate the child.

In a number of States the expense of confinement is made a part of the judgment. They include Arizona, Arkansas, Connecticut, Delaware, Florida, Georgia, Maine, Maryland, Massachusetts, Minnesota, New Jersey, New York, Oregon, Pennsylvania, Rhode Island, and Wisconsin.

Period of Support. The time during which the father may be required to make payments toward the support of the child is specified only in about one-third of the States. It ranges up to 18 years. In Arkansas it is 7 years; in Alabama, Florida, and Illinois, 10 years; in South Dakota, 11 years; in Maryland, 12 years; in the District of Columbia, Georgia, and Oregon, 14 years; in Delaware, 15 years; in Wisconsin, 16 years; in Colorado, Mississippi, and Utah, 18 years or less. In Kentucky, as noted above, the jury determines the time, and in Vermont, West Virginia, and North Dakota the payments may be continued as long as the judge thinks the child may need them for support.

Enforcement. The problem of enforcement of judgments rendered in support cases is one of peculiar difficulty. A large proportion of the defendants are relatively irresponsible, without property or assured income. The period of support is usually a long one, and it is seldom indeed that regular payments are made over its full term. Neverthel ss many factors are making for more stringent fulfillment of the court's decree. One of the chief difficulties is that the offending father may go to another State, from which there may be legal bars to bringing him back. One of the objects of having a uniform law adopted among the several States is to make it easier to reach him through civil action in the State to which he has fled.

All things considered, the procedure for enforcement outlined in the Uniform Act represents probably the most effective method of holding the father to his duty of providing support. Under this procedure the court, after giving judgment, may require the father to give bond for the making of the designated payments. If he does not or can not give such bond he may be put in jail for a year, after which he may be discharged as an insolvent debtor, although he still remains liable to pay the judgment. Instead of putting him in jail, or after releasing him from jail, the court may commit him to the custody of a probation officer and require him to make whatever payments and reports seem advisable, and if he fails to comply with these orders he may be committed or recommitted to jail.

If he does give bond, and later defaults in making any payment called for by the court's judgment, his bond may be forfeited and he may be held in contempt of court, subject to commitment to jail in the same manner as if he had failed to give bond.

The great advantage of this proposed measure lies in the fact that, in the first place, the court maintains legal control over the father while the judgment runs, with power to send him to jail for default, and in the second place it may keep in close touch with him through the probation officer. In a large number of cases the ability to make the payments ordered depends on the man's day-to-day earning power. It is of no particular benefit to any one concerned to keep him in jail, except in the occasional State where his prison earnings are applied to meeting his debt. But it is useful to have the threat of jail hanging over his head, with the eye of the court, through the probation officer, always upon him, while through his earnings he maintains his ability to satisfy the judgment.

This method obviously works only so long as the father remains in the jurisdiction of the court, or subject to be returned to it. What of the absconding father who crosses the State line? He can not be extradited unless he is a fugitive from justice, and he is not such fugitive unless the commission of some crime is involved. Several States have attempted to meet this situation by making different actions or non-actions of the father criminal offenses—Pennsylvania, the act of illicit intercourse, and also the non-support of the illegitimate child; the

New England States, the begetting of an illegitimate child; California, Colorado, Connecticut, Delaware, and other States, the abandonment of the illegitimate as well as the legitimate child; and Minnesota, the act of absconding, under certain conditions, itself. To all these there are serious objections, although they apply more particularly to the absconding defendant before rather than after paternity is legally fixed. The Uniform Act proposes, rather experimentally, to reach the absconding father through both criminal and civil action, the former by making failure to carry out a support judgment, or failure to support his illegitimate child not in his custody, a misdemeanor, and the latter by permitting proceedings to compel support to be brought wherever the father is permanently or temporarily resident, or wherever th mother or the child resides, or is found. Suit may be brought even though mother and child are residents of another State. It is also provided that a judgment for support obtained in one State may be sued upon in another and be made a domestic judgment. The efficacy of these measures clearly increases rapidly as more and more States adopt them.

In existing laws nearly all the States have the principal enforcement feature of the Uniform Act. This is the provision that the father must give bond for the making of the payments ordered by the court, and on failure to do so may be committed to jail for varying periods, being released eventually as an insolvent debtor, but not being relieved of the support obligation. The length of such maximum confinement varies considerably. In Alabama it is one year at hard labor. In Florida, Indiana, Kansas, South Dakota, and Utah it is also one one year, while Maryland imposes two years. In Connecticut, the District of Columbia, Maine, Michigan, Mississippi, and Vermont the period is six months; in Arizona, Minnesota, Ohio, Wisconsin, and Wyoming, three months; in Massachusetts, two months. Many States provide merely that the defendant shall be discharged as insolvent on proved inability to pay. California makes it permissible to employ him on public works, payment for which up to $1.50 a day is applied to the child's support. Georgia makes failure to give bond a misdemeanor, with the fine going to the maintenance of the child.

In one State, Iowa, the courts have held that imprisonment for failure to make these support payments is contrary to the constitutional prohibition against imprisonment for debt. Most States, however, have either not passed on the question or have decided the penalty to be constitutional. The Iowa procedure of levying against any property the defendant may have is also followed by several other States.

Compromise. Release of the defendant from all further liability for support through the making of a money settlement with the mother is a common practice. It differs, however, from the usual settlement of civil disputes through compromise in that the State is necessarily an interested party because of its concern for the support of the child. In two States the minimum amount of such settlement is specified (Illinois, $400; Iowa, $500), and in nearly all the others the compromise must have the sanction of the court. Nevada flatly prohibits any settlement merely by the father and mother. As a rule, however, a compromise arrived at between the father and mother is deemed acceptable, provided the court considers it reasonably adequate for the maintenance of the child.

As noted above the Uniform Act attempts to guard against an abuse of the compromise principle by declaring that no such agreement is binding on the mother and child unless "adequate provision is fully secured by payment or otherwise" and unless it is approved by a court having jurisdiction to compel support of the child.

STATUS PROVISIONS

The question of the status of the illegitimate child before the law is immensely important both because of the practical consequences which flow from it, and because it bears so strongly upon its future social consciousness. It involves questions as to when a child is to be considered illegitimate, how it may be made legitimate, and its legal relations to its parents and to society.

In general the tendency of modern times has been toward a lightening of the disabilities resulting on the illegitimate child. Slowly the sheer cruelty and injustice of visiting on the head of an individual the penalty for an act for which he is in not the slightest degree responsible is becoming recognized in the public consciousness, and this attitude is being reflected in the laws. Under the British and American common law the illegitimate child was a legal outcast. In England the status continues to be determined by the common law, but in this country there has from the start been legislation altering his legal status as well as providing for his support. Virginia led off with legislation in 1785, introducing the three reforms of making the issue of certain annulled marriages legitimate, providing for legitimation by subsequent marriage, and providing that mother and child should inherit from each other. Most States have incorporated these provisions in their codes. In recent years there has been considerable interest in the question of status, both in

Europe and in this country, and one or two States have gone far toward taking away all legal disabilities from the illegitimate child.

What Children Are Legitimate. All children born in wedlock are presumed by the law generally to be legitimate, and this presumption holds even in cases where divorce is granted for adultery of the wife so far as children begotten before the offense are concerned. A number of States, including California, Montana, North Dakota, South Dakota, Oklahoma, and Louisiana, provide that children born within ten months after dissolution of marriage shall be presumed to be legitimate.

Children born of marriages which are annulled, such as those found to be violating the laws against bigamy or incest, as well as cases of ordinary divorce, are usually held to be legitimate. Iowa, Kentucky, Maine, Massachusetts, New Hampshire, and Wyoming regard the issue of incestuous marriages as illegitimate, and a few States include the issue of bigamous marriages in the same cliass. In cases of divorce on the grounds of antenuptial pregnancy the issue is illegitimate in several States, but in practically all other cases divorce of parents does not affect legitimacy of children.

Legitimation of Illegitimate Children. Practically all States have specific provisions of law legitimating illegitmate children through the subsequent marriage of their parents, but a large proportion append the condition that the child shall be recog-nized by the father. The latter requirement is made by Arkansas, California, the District of Columbia, Georgia, Illinois, Indiana, Massachusetts, Michigan, Mississippi, Missouri, Nebraska, New Jersey, New York, North Dakota, Ohio, Texas, Vermont, Washington, West Virginia, and Wyoming. Ne-

THE CARE OF THE UNMARRIED MOTHER

braska requires not only that the father shall recognize the child, but that the parents shall also have other issue. South Dakota provides for legitimation by subsequent marriage, but makes acknowledgment by the father necessary to inheritance rights.

Legitimation without the marriage of the parents is provided for in a considerable number of States. Often this is accomplished by public acknowledgment and adoption of the child into the father's family, sometimes by court order in response to the father's petition. In some cases informal adoption is held to legitimate the child by the specific language of the statute. In others, however, its legal status is not so definitely determined.

Abandonment Statutes. The question of sta us is important, among other respects, with regard to the protection of the illegitimate child by statutes forbidding the abandonment of dependent children. A few States expressly include illegitimate children among those to whom the law applies. These States are Colorado, Delaware, Massachusetts, Nebraska, West Virginia, and Wisconsin.

Legal Relation to Parents. Practically all States expressly provide by statute for the inheritance by illegitimate children from their mother, in case she dies intestate, but the simple right is occasionally hedged about with modifications. In Idaho the illegitimate child does not represent mother or father by inheriting any estate of their kindred. In Massachusetts it inherits from the mother and any maternal ancestor. In Michigan it inherits from but not through the mother, and the same is true in North Carolina, except that it may not take land left to the mother by the father of her legitimate children. In

Wisconsin, Washington, Oklahoma, Oregon, South Dakota, Nebraska, and Montana the illegitimate child inherits from his mother, but does not represent her in matters of inheritance unless it has been legitimated by subsequent marriage of its parents. In all cases the mother enjoys the right of inheritance from her illegitimate child if the latter dies without issue, and transmits this right to her next of kin.

The Louisiana laws relating to illegitimacy are unique with respect to matters of inheritance as well as other phases of the subject. They distinguish between illegitimate children whose parents might legally have married and those whose parents could not have married. The former, when acknowledged by their father, are designated as natural children. Natural children inherit from their mother only if she has acknowledged them and has left no lawful descendants. If she has left such descendants the natural children receive only moderate alimony. Illegitimates born from adulterous or incestuous union do not inherit from either parent, and are allowed only alimony. Children who inherit from their natural parents can come into possession only through court order. They do not inherit through either parent.

The rights of inheritance of illegitimate children from their fathers are decidedly involved. No such right obtains, of course, in the absence of acknowledgement of paternity or of its establishment through court action. In States which specifically set forth a method of legitimation it is sometimes stated that this action bestows on the child the full rights of legitimate-born children. In others the right of inheritance is modified. A number of States provide for legitimation through informal adoption, but the precise rights of inheritance are not always made clear. In such cases court decisions must be depended upon to establish the rights of a given child. Whenever the question may arise in connection with the work of aiding unmarried mothers it will be advisable to obtain a legal opinion based upon an examination of the laws and decisions of the given State.

The chief legal relation of the father to the child, aside from the question of status (which, however, also involves the question of support), rests in his obligation to support it as set forth in the statutes. California law makes the failure of the father to support and educate his illegitimate child a crime. In Delaware and Massachusetts such non-support is declared a misdemeanor, and in Oregon it is a misdemeanor for a man to fail to support a child while he lived with its mother unless he affirmatively shows it is not his child. For the most part, however, the laws content themselves simply with the statement that the father is charged with the duty of supporting the child, thus laying the basis for quasi-criminal actions for non-support.

ADOPTION LAWS

Although present sentiment among social workers strongly favors keeping the illegitimate child with its mother wherever possible, a proportion of such infants will no doubt always have to be taken care of by adoption. It can not be emphasized too strongly that such adoption should always be in accordance with the procedure laid down by law. This means in nearly all States that the action will have to be taken through the aid of a court. At the very least, such procedure insures the future legal status of the child. Under more recent advanced legislation and practice it will also probably mean that the antecedents of the child and the circumstances of the adopting family are carefully investigated. Much of the disappointment and distress that too often result from the placing of children by unscrupulous professionals will thus be avoided.

The process of adoption through the court is practically the same in essentials everywhere. It consists of a petition to the proper court by the persons wishing to adopt a child; notice to the child's parents, or to properly authorized persons acting in place of the parents; their consent; and the final order of court transferring the child. Until recent times this was all too often little more than a formality. Now it is coming to imply the exercise of a special interest by the State in the welfare of the child, and the interest can be made effective where the court is associated with social agencies.

The most notable feature of later legislation among the States is the increasing insistence on full investigation of child and foster parents, for the protection of both, and a general State supervision over the process of adoption and the subsequent welfare of the child. Some States, Minnesota and North Dakota for example, go so far as to forbid adoption of children under specified ages except by court order.[1]

New Jersey forbids the offering of a child through the public press for adoption without prior notification of the proper State authority. Michigan makes the written approval by the county agent of a proposed home into which the child is to be adopted a prerequisite for such adoption of a child under seventeen.

Several States give particular attention to adoption from maternity homes and lying-in hospitals. Illinois provides that

---

[1] See "Adoption Laws of the United States," by Emelyn Foster Peck, U. S. Children's Bureau Publicaton No. 148.

no child shall be placed in a family home (or be legally adopted) until such home shall be investigated and approved by the State board of administration. In Alabama no relative of an illegitimate child, except its mother, may take it from a maternity institution without the written consent of the court, and in Connecticut the child can be surrendered by the institution only to some one having a legal right to receive it. Statutes of similar purport in other States show that the public mind is increasingly aware of the need for close supervision over the much-abused practices of adoption.

CRIMINAL LAWS.

In the realm of law the chief interest of the agency worker will naturally lie in the civil codes, since it is through them that aid to the mother is to be obtained from the father, if at all, through legal process. But some knowledge of the statutes relating to sex crimes will at times also be found most useful. Rescue homes are peculiarly in a position to gauge the social and personal results of sexual criminality. Often they obtain information concerning particular offenders which is broached to no one else. It is a duty to society to make full use of this information to protect future innocence from attack by helping to put behind the bars the perpetrators of past crimes.

The classification of crimes against sex offers certain difficulties in that several factors enter in which are hardly capable of precise definition. The difference between a felony (capital crime) and a misdemeanor is sometimes slight. The mental competency of the victim of assault, the intent of the offender, the attitude of the girl or woman, the previous moral character of the complainant and her reputation in the community, are some of the factors which determined the seriousness of a crime and make its proper punishment a difficult problem for judge or jury.

The statutes of the various States cover about the same offenses and the distinctions between the various grades of offense are much the same, but there is considerable range in the penalties assessed. Legislation in the newer States of the West tend to more elaborate and detailed definitions than, say, in the New England or the Southern States.

Prostitution, with its attendant crimes such as pandering, procuring, enticing into immoral life, etc.; adultery; incest; rape in various forms; sex crimes against children; seduction; abduction; and other offenses against decency and morality, covering the whole gamut from a slight misdemeanor to a capital crime, receive attention in the code of every State. It would lie outside our province to discuss in detail the provisions of these various laws. It will be sufficient here to take up a few phases of the subject which commonly come to the attention of agency workers.

Age of Consent. When a boy or man is charged with a sexual offense against a young girl, the question whether the girl was above or below the "age of consent" becomes of first importance. In its broader sense "the age of censent" is a legal term meaning the age at which the law considers a person competent to give assent to a proposal or action of his own free will. Thus there is an "age of consent" for marriage. But in common usage the phrase is taken as applying specifically to cases of unlawful sexual intercourse. In this narrower sense it usually means the age at which a young girl understands the nature of the sexual act, and is old enough to bear the responsibility of giving or withholding her consent. It is fixed by both common and statutory law. Its special legal importance lies in the fact that offenses against girls under the age of consent are considered a form of rape and are severely punished.

In modern times there has been a strong tendency to raise the age of consent. Formerly it was unbelievably low—at the common law only ten years, and in many States but little higher. Today in most States it is at least well within the bounds of reason. Almost all States now specify an age of consent of 16 or 18 years, as shown in the following list:

12 years	New Mexico	Mississippi
Alabama	North Carolina	Missouri
Hawaii	Ohio	Montana
	Pennsylvania	Nebraska
14 years	South Carolina	Nevada
Georgia	Vermont	New York
Porto Rico	Virginia	North Dakota
	West Virginia	Oklahoma
16 years		Oregon
Arkansas	*18 years*	Rhode Island
Connecticut	Arizona	South Dakota
District of Columbia	California	Texas
Illinois	Colorado	Utah
Indiana	Delaware	Washington
Iowa	Florida	Wisconsin
Maine	Idaho	Wyoming
Maryland	Kansas	
Massachusetts	Kentucky	*21 years*
Michigan	Louisiana	Tennessee
New Hampshire	Minnesota	
New Jersey		

There are a number of minor qualifications to the list. In Alabama, for instance, a heavy penalty attaches for offenses against a girl between twelve and sixteen years, except where the offender is himself under sixteen. In some States the age limit is lowered in cases where the girl was not of chaste character before the offense—in Florida to 10 years, in Mississippi, North Carolina, and Tennessee to 12 years, in Texas to 15 years, and in Missouri, Nebraska, Oklahoma, Oregon, and Rhode Island to 16 years[1]. In almost half the States there can be no conviction for sexual offenses when the male is under a specified age.

Rape. Practically all States distinguish between at least two classes of rape, one of the violation of any female through force and against her will, and the other, known as "statutory rape," consisting of intercourse with any girl, with or without her consent, who is below the legal age of consent. Several States have gone much further in defining the offense. Typical of the law of several States is the following classification from the laws of North Dakota:

"Rape is an act of sexual intercourse, accomplished with a female not the wife of the perpetrator, under any of the following circumstances:

"1. When the female is under the age of 18 years.

"2. When she is incapable, through lunacy or any other unsoundness of mind, whether temporary or permanent, of giving legal consent.

"3. When she resists, but her resistance is overcome by force or violence.

"4. When she is prevented from resisting, by threats of immediate and great bodily harm, accompanied by apparent power of execution.

"5. When she is prevented from resisting by an intoxicating, narcotic, or anesthetic agent, administered by or with the privity of the accused.

"6. When she is at the time unconscious of the nature of the act, and this is known to the accused.

"7. When she submits under the belief that the person committing the act is her husband, and this belief is induced by artifice, pretense, or concealment practiced by the accused, with intent to induce such belief."

---

[1] Dr. George B. Mangold calls attention to the fact that in some of the states, especially in Missouri, where the 18-age limit applies, the law is practically inoperative for girls above 15 years because of the qualifications. He says the actual previous chastity of the girl has but little to do with the result.

Three degrees of the crime are recognized, the differences being largely differences of age of the accused. Idaho, Colorado, and Indiana likewise punish rape in more than one degree.

The death penalty for committing rape holds in eighteen States, the District of Columbia, and Hawaii, with alternatives of imprisonment for life or for specified periods. The States included in the list are Alabama, Arkansas, Delaware, Florida, Georgia, Kentucky, Louisiana, Maryland, Mississippi, Missouri, Nevada, North Carolina, Oklahoma, South Carolina, Tennessee, Texas, Virginia, and West Virginia. Life imprisonment as a maximum penalty is provided by Arizona, Colorado, Idaho, Illinois, Iowa, Massachusetts, Michigan, and Wyoming. Kansas imposes five to twenty-one years at hard labor, California a maximum of fifty years, Maine "any term of years," Massachusetts and Iowa "life or any term of years," etc.

Seduction. Nearly all States have a statute providing punishment for seduction. Except for variations in the age limit it is in substance practically the same everywhere. The crime comes under this heading when a man obtains access to a girl under a specified age limit, usually 18, under promise to marry her, and then fails to do so. It applies only when the girl was of chaste character or repute before the offense.

In nearly all States the uncorroborated testimony of the girl herself is insufficient to convict on a charge of seduction. A favorite penalty among the different States is one to ten years imprisonment, sometimes with further provision for a fine. In practically all States the law provides that if the accused shall marry the girl before judgment is passed such action shall be a bar to further prosecution. In some States, however, the prosecution is merely suspended by the marriage, and is revived if the husband deserts his wife within a specified time, usually three to five years, without the cause which would entitle him to a divorce.

Action for damages can be brought as a civil case by the girl, and in some State codes it is provided that such suits may also be brought by the father (or in case of his death, desertion or imprisonment, by the mother), or by the guardian, even though the girl was not living with any of these persons when the offense was committed and it did not cause them to lose her services.

OBJECTIVES OF LEGAL ACTION.

The objects to be achieved by a resort to the courts on the part of the unmarried mother may be listed chiefly as (1) the establishment of paternity; (2) support of child provided by regular payments, which may also include costs of confinement and payment of other expenses; (3) effecting of a compromise, by which usually a specified sum is paid to the mother, presumably for the support of the child; (4) marriage.

The first three of these results have been sufficiently discussed. But a word should be said with regard to forced marriages. The usual assumption is that this is the most desirable settlement of all. It makes the child legitimate, "gives it a name," relieves the mother of the social outlawry she might otherwise suffer, and establishes a family. But it would not be wise to forget that these advantages may be partly balanced by other results not so happy.

In a special study of 133 marriages contracted by unmarried mothers it was found that within one year after the marriages took place nearly one-third of the girls had encountered non-support, desertion, or divorce. It is not always a solution of the difficulties of an unmarried mother to be joined in wedlock with the man who happens to be the father of her child, but who may also be dissolute or othrewise of bad character. Here the social worker can help out by undertaking an investigation of the prospective husband and determining from her findings what will be the chances of a successful marriage, and if they are unfavorable whether the advantages of such an alliance will after all outweigh the disadvantages.

CHAPTER SIX
KEEPING MOTHER AND CHILD TOGETHER

In the development of means to help the unmarried mother and her child, no plan has gained greater headway in recent years than that which provides that in practically all cases the mother and child should not be separated, but should be kept together as a family unit, incomplete though it may be. More than forty years ago the wisdom of this procedure was recognized by Dr. Kate Waller Barrett, one of the founders of the National Florence Crittenton Mission. Dr. Barrett, in a paper "Motherhood as a Means of Regeneration," declared:

There are three interests to be considered, the mother's, the child's, and society's.

It is best for the mother that she rear her own child, because the child gives her an interest in life. A woman who has trusted her all to one man, and has been deceived, and finds herself under the ban of society, is in a deplorably lonely position. All the opportunities and most of the ties of her past life have fallen away from her. Just now she must have a new motive in life. If, in pursuing the plain path of duty, she can have a motive of love and self-interest, as well as of duty, to give color and aim to her in life, one of the most important factors for her happiness and usefulness has been found. The rewards of motherhood are the most blessed hopes in every woman's life who has tasted the joys of motherhood, and why should not the poor girl who has nothing else to live for at least have that sweet consolation? How often do I hear beautiful, talented girls in our homes say: "If it wasn't for my child I would not want to live; but having him, my life is full of happiness."

The influence of the nursery in the progress of right living is not the training that the child gets there so much as it is the training that the mother gets there. Our girls need the influence of the child-life upon them. They need to have the qualities that are essential to a strong, well-regulated character trained in them. This can better be accomplished through the children than in any other way. So often, when I have seen the wonderful regenerating influence that has come to a girl through motherhood—how the selfishness and shallowness and self-will have all vanished, how in asking wisdom of God as to how she shall train her child she has learned how to control herself—with what new force and meaning I recalled that verse which, in times past, has been somewhat of a broken promise, when we think of those who have given up their lives in giving birth to their children: "She shall be saved in childbearing." Yes, saved; not from physical death only, but from what is far worse, spiritual death.

It is best for the child to be reared by its own mother. If a child is not cared for by its mother, it must either be sent to some institution, or else be adopted into some family or taken "to be raised," as they say. The number of persons competent to raise children are few at best, and many of these have children of their own. The majority of homes that are open to illegitimate children are not as a rule the best homes in a community. Most persons adopting children do so in the hope of having servants that will not cost them wages. We can recall but few children that we have known to be adopted that were particularly well reared. The number of thinking persons who have had much to do with child-saving is increasing who agree that institutional life is very bad for fitting children for the battle of life. Many of the girls who are today in our Florence Crittenton Homes have been reared in Christian orphan asylums, many of them under apparently the best surroundings, and many others were adopted children.

The cause of the failure of institutions for children lies in the fact that the children are reared up into automatons instead of thinking and reasoning beings. They have had every question decided for them, and have had good forced upon them; they have not chosen it. The natural tendencies have been held in check by rules, but will not have been eradicated. Their every want has been supplied without any effort or anxiety on their part, and there have been none of the makeshifts of poverty that have played so large a part in moulding the character of the men who have in turn moulded the destinies of the world. Their individuality is not considered. There is but little attention given to developing strength of character. They own nothing of their own, not even a toy to play with. Just at the time they need a watchful hand, they are turned loose, put into some family or position, and left to choose their own course in life. It is but little wonder that they so readily fall a victim to the seducer's words of honeyed poison. They hunger for individual love and companionship. Next to an incubator-hatched chicken, I think an institution-reared child seems most abnormal, and deserves the sympathy of those who know what it is to have a home. In many instances, the persons placed in charge of children in institutions have no children of their own and often are not suited for the work. I have seen a child taken from a mother because it was agreed that she was not competent to take charge of it and placed in the hands of another woman who was just as incompetent to fill the requirements of a mother. The only difference was that the other woman was paid to do what the mother would have so willingly done for love.

It is best for society that the mother and child be kept together. Society is so complex in its organization that when one member suffers the whole body suffers with it. It can not afford to overlook its lowliest member, even the illegitimate child and its disinherited mother, upon the grounds of self-preservation. It is for the good of the society that as soon as a member becomes diseased or injured it be quickly healed so that it may properly perform the duties that are accorded it. The sooner an abnormal member becomes normal the better it is for all the members. A child reared by its mother in some semblance of a home is in a better condition to regain its normal attitude toward the world at large than one reared in any other way.

God has mercifully fulfilled His promise to those the world would disinherit, according to His promise in Isaiah 56:5; "Even unto them will I give in mine house, and in my walls a place and a name better than sons and daughters." The names of illegitimate children have made bright the pages of history, poetry, art, and music. Their names have been the battle cry that has led armies on to victory, and empires have been conquered under their banner. They have held the highest places in Church and State. In no department of progress have they not done their part in the great onward march. And, above all, thousands have gone before to glory to make glad the City of God. But when we study the history of those who, in the face of every obstacle the blind prejudice of the world has heaped in their path, have been able to surmount all difficulties and force the world to recognize their intrinsic worth, we do not find that they were given over into the hands of others to raise. The annals of foundling asylums and other public institutions are lamentably wanting in any glorious record of the achievements of those whom they have sheltered and for whom they have done all that any institution could do to fit them for the battle of life. No: it was always the mother's hand that led these trembling, stumbling feet to victory. 'Twas she who bared her breast to the slings and arrows of the world in order that her child might have her tender care.

I am glad to say that the plan of keeping the mother and child together is now advised by every prominent rescue worker of broad experience in the world. Josephine Butler, whose name is known throughout the world for her labors in behalf of the liberty of women who are defrauded of their rights, says that in all her experiences she has never found a single case where she thought mother and child should be separated; that often she had made up her mind to do so, but after a trial, had come back to feel that it is not child-saving we are after alone, but mother-saving also, and that what is good for the mother can not be bad for the child.

In considering this question, we must remember how necessary the influence of motherhood is to the world, what it has done for the world in the past, and what consecrated motherhood will do for the world in the future if it is only cultivated and developed. Scientists show us that all that is best and truest in civilization is due to it. Our beautiful homes are but the outgrowth of the rock caves where the prehistoric mother took refuge during the period of gestation and lactation; to her we owe the taming of the milk-giving animals that were necessary to give food to her offspring; our gardens are the outgrowth of the little patches of cereals which were first cultivated for the food of these animals. Through the mother, the ties of kindred were first established and united family life made possible. The succession of pro erty and titles were first through her, until laws were made to decide the certainty of paternity, for while doubt may be thrown upon the fatherhood of *any* child, the mother-hood is always established without any doubt whatever. We can not afford in any way to lessen this wonderful influence of motherhood. We must not forget that motherhood is motherhood *per se;* that there is no difference in the reflex action of motherhood, whether it be legal or illegal. A mother loves one child as well as she does another, the illegitimate child is just as dear as the legitimate child, and certainly, if she had the power of making laws, she would not disinherit the weaker for the stronger. That is not woman's way of doing. If you would go into our homes and see there the mothers holding tightly to their little ones, and see the anxious solicitude with which they watch the tendencies of their children, trying to protect them from inherent weakness, you would know that we are training a race of ideal mothers from those you have thought unworthy to take care of their own children. When I recall the many girls that I have known in past years who have been faithful to their children and are now living with them, honored members of their children's households, I feel that the faithfulness of the mother has wiped out the curse of the father. According to Jeremiah 31:29: "They shall say no more, 'Thy fathers have eaten a sour grape, and the children's teeth are set on edge'." God is able to bring in play a higher law than even heredity, and that is the law of redemption through Jesus Christ our Lord.

In the foregoing statement, we would not seem arbitrary, nor state that there are no circumstances that would justify the giving up of children by their mothers, but it does seem as if philanthropic workers should not put a premium upon unfaithfulness as they sometimes seem to do. Surely no one should have the authority to separate mother and child who has not had wide experience and also a genius for homemaking.

Keeping mother and child together has been one of the fundamental principles of Florence Crittenton work ever since it was established, and at the 44th annual conference held in Nashville, Tenn., May 1-3, 1927, the following resolution was adopted:

Whereas, the founder of our work laid great emphasis upon the importance of keeping mother and child together, and whereas this principle is now approved by the best informed public opinion, as is shown by utterances of experts in social service and by legislation in a number of States, be it resolved, That we reaffirm our belief that Crittenton Homes should make every effort in each individual case to work out a plan by which mother and baby may be kept together.[1]

Dr. Barrett has given in her paper referred to the strongest reasons why the mother and child should be kept together from the standpoint of the mother, but other authorities have come to the same conclusions because of the effects upon the child. These conclusions have been reached largely through the study of mortality rates for infants born out of wedlock. European statistics have shown that mortality among such infants is invariably higher than among other infants, sometimes more than twice as high. The rather meager statistics upon this subject in the United States show a similar situation.

A study made in Boston covering the year 1914 showed a death rate for infants of illegitimate birth three times as high as the rate for infants born in wedlock; in New Bedford in

[1] Annual report National Florence Crittenton Mission, 1926, page 63.

1913 and Milwaukee in 1916-17 the rates were, respectively, 2.7 times and 2.3 times as high. In Baltimore in 1915 the infant mortality rate for white infants born out of wedlock was 3.3 times as high as the rate for other white infants, and among the colored infants the difference in the rates was 1.8. Marked improvement has taken place in some of these cities in recent years. In Baltimore in 1921 the rate for white infants of illegitimate birth was only 1.8 times as high as the rate for other white infants, and the rates for colored infants of legitimate and illegitimate birth were practically equal.[1]

Perhaps the most important factor in high infant mortality is early separation of the mother and child and the consequent difficulties with feeding. A sentiment growing in favor in many communities is that of keeping mother and child together wherever the mother's rights and obligations and the welfare of the child can be promoted by this means. The policy of keeping mother and child together, at least during the nursing period, has been advocated for a long time and has been followed successfully by many maternity homes and by some child-caring agencies.

The higher death rate among infants artificially fed than among those breast fed has directed attention to the influence of the type of feeding on infant mortality, and has been responsible for much of the change in public opinion that now stresses the importance of keeping mother and child together. Thirty-two States have promoted breast feeding through talks by the State staff or advice given at conferences, through special literature, charts, films, and pictures on the subject, and through

---

[1] "Illegitimacy as a Child-Welfare Problem," Children's Bureau Publication No. 66. Washington, 1920.

advice given by nurses in visits to the homes of expectant mothers and of mothers of newborn babies. The general educational work has included instruction of mothers as to the importance of keeping the baby on his mother's milk, and as to methods of maintaining her supply of milk. Several States have conducted breast-feeding surveys and campaigns.

Recent legislation in three States has given legal sanction to the policy of requiring mothers and babies to remain together during the nursing period. Maryland public sentiment was aroused by a study made by the State vice commission in 1914, which revealed the seriousness of the problem of early separation from their mothers of infants born out of wedlock and the high mortality prevailing among babies cared for in institutions apart from their mothers. In 1916 a statute was enacted providing that no child under six months of age may be separated from his mother for placement in a foster home or institution except under one of the three following specified conditions: (1) Certification (with statement of the reasons for the necessity of separation for the physical good of the mother or child) by two physicians qualified to practice medicine in the State of Maryland and engaged in active practice for at least five years; (2) order for separation by a court of competent jurisdiction; (3) written consent to separation by the board of State aid and charities. The law makes no distinction between children born out of wedlock and children of legitimate birth, but in operation it affects mainly children of illegitimate birth. North Carolina enacted in 1917 a statute similar to that of Maryland forbidding separation except with the written consent of the clerk of the superior court and of the county health officer. South Carolina passed a law in 1923 (applicable only to counties of 90,000 to 100,000 inhabitants) making it unlawful to remove a baby under six months of age from the mother for the purpose of placing in a foster home without the written consent of the judge of the children's court and the county health officer, and in 1924 passed a law requiring that persons, agencies, or organizations removing from his mother a child under six months of age report to the child-placing bureau of the State board of public welfare the names and addresses of the persons taking the child and of the parents of the child. This requirement does not apply in case the child is known to have been born in wedlock.

In order to ascertain, if possible, the effect of the Maryland law upon mortality among infants born out of wedlock and upon the policies and work of social agencies, the United States Children's Bureau made a study in Baltimore of conditions in the year 1921. One of the bureau's infant mortality studies had covered babies born in Baltimore in 1915 (the year before the passage of the law) so that comparable data for this earlier period were available.

According to findings of the bureau's study, infant mortality among babies born out of wedlock has been markedly reduced in Baltimore, both absolutely and in relation to mortality among children of legitimate birth. Approximately 1 in every 3 infants born out of wedlock in 1915 died before the age of one year, and 1 in every 4 before the age of six months. Of the babies born in 1921 only 1 in every 8 died before the first birthday and only 1 in every 12 before six months. Mortality among infants born out of wedlock was reduced more than 50 per cent between 1915 and 1921, and the rate for infants of legitimate birth was reduced less than 20 per cent. In 1915 the mortality rate among infants born out of wedlock was almost three times as high as the corresponding rate for infants of legitimate birth; in 1921 it was one and one-half times as high. The percentage of decrease in the mortality rate among infants of illegitimate birth was greater (80.4 per cent) for babies of 1 to 3 months than for any other age period.

In Minnesota, under a joint resolution adopted in July, 1918, by the State board of health and the board of control, hospitals and maternity homes must require their patients to nurse infants at the breast so long as they remain under the care of the institution. Where nursing by the mother is impossible for any physical reason exception to this rule may be made by the State board of health or State board of control acting upon proper medical advice.

The Milwaukee program for keeping mothers and babies together during a three-months' nursing period was put into effect in 1919. In the two-year period, 1916-17, the mortality rate in Milwaukee for infants born out of wedlock was 236.8, or 2.3 times the rate for children of legitimate birth. A study of illegitimacy covering the year ended September 30, 1917, showed that more than half the children included in the study had been separated from their mothers, and that 45 per cent of the children whose ages at the time of the first separation were known had been separated within a month after birth. The executive secretary of the Juvenile Protective Association, in describing the results of Milwaukee's program for unmarried mothers and babies after it had been two years in operation, commented as follows:

The results of these measures have been gratifying and far-reaching. The child-placing organizations and the doctors and other individuals who for-

[97]

merly brought many babies a few days old into the city to be placed for adoption are now required to have permits to board them until they are placed with adoptive parents. Commercial lying-in hospitals and maternity homes, which formerly permitted mothers to leave when their babies were only 10 days or two weeks old, without any effort at breast feeding, must now apply for a permit to keep the babies without the mother. This requirement gives an opportunity for a social investigation, and for finding a way to keep the mother and baby together, in the city or elsewhere, during the three months' nursing period.

Under the Milwaukee plan, application for separation or from exemption from the three months' breast-feeding rule is submitted to the Juvenile Protective Association. A study of applicants for separation during the first eight months showed that 69 per cent of those who applied for immediate separation were persuaded to keep their babies and nurse them, and only 9 per cent of this group released their children at the end of three months. It has been the experience of the association that the appeal to the unmarried mother to nurse her baby at least for the minimum period of three months, as a kind of reparation for having brought him into the world so handicapped, is an almost unfailing argument. It has been found also that at the end of the period, not only has there been an opportunity for a thorough social investigation, but the mother has had a chance to recover from her physical and mental strain and is more capable of deciding what she wishes to do for her baby and for her own rehabilitation.

Striking proof of the saving of infant life which results from keeping mother and child together under proper conditions during part or all of the nursing period is shown by the following study made in Boston by the United States Children's Bureau.

PER CENT OF INFANTS BORN OUT OF WEDLOCK IN 1914, WHO DIED DURING THEIR
FIRST YEAR OF LIFE, BY PLACE OF BIRTH

Place of birth	Infants born out wedlock 1914	Deaths known to have occured in first year of life	
		Number	Per Cent
Total	847	230	27.2
Private home	193	46	23.8
Hospital	410	144	35.1
Large maternity hospital and children's institution	209	94	45.0
Other hospital	201	50	24.9
Maternity home	241	40	16.6
Note reported	3	—	—

The highest percentage of deaths occurred among infants born in hospitals, and the lowest among those born in maternity homes. The large number of deaths among those born in hospitals is probably due to the fact that hospitals usually keep mother and child for only a short period following the child's birth, and after discharge from the hospital the infant often is separated from the mother. The proportion of mothers who do not keep their infants is probably larger among those who are confined in hospitals than among those confined in the homes of relatives or friends. However, the percentage of deaths among infants born in hospitals other than the large maternity hospital and children's institution specified was very little higher than the percentage among infants born in private homes—25 as compared with 24.

The plan of keeping mother and child together presents many difficulties to those who are interested in the future of the unmarried woman and her child born out of wedlock, but the writer is of the opinion that at least two general principles should be adopted by those who deal with this difficult problem:

First, the mother should be urged to feed her baby from the

breast for such period of time as will give the baby a start in life. Such a period of time should in no instance be less than six months, and in the great majority of cases should not be less than nine months.

Second, no plans for the separation of mother and child after the above period should be made until after all the circumstances of the girl's history, as well as those of the putative father, have been investigated, and it is definitely shown that the separation is for the best interest of both the mother and the child. The writer believes that the greatest possible caution should be used in reaching this decision, and that it is better to try out one or more plans for keeping the mother and child together and have them fail and then agree to the separation rather than agree in the first instance.

There are several means by which a more or less complete adjustment of the mother and child to society may be made.[1]

1. The parents may marry each other and establish a home for the child. If a normal home life results, the greater part of the handicap of illegitimate birth is removed.

2. The mother may marry another man and the child be accepted as a member of the family. Here, so far as physical care is concerned, the conditions under which the child is brought up closely approximate those surrounding children of legitimate birth. Certain detrimental factors may develop, however, in the "stepfather family," such as a jealous or scornful attitude on the part of the half brothers and sisters, or discrimination on the part of the stepfather in favor of his own children.

3. The mother, though not establishing a home as a result of marriage, may keep the child with her, either in the home of

---

[1] "Illegitimacy as a Child-Welfare Problem," Vol. 2, page 147.

her relatives, in her place of employment, or in an independent home which she maintains. The difficulties are often very great, and the result for the child may be fortunate or unfortunate according to the character of the mother and her ability to support the child. Often the mother is obliged to depend upon social agencies for financial and other assistance. In any case the child lacks the advantages of normal family life.

4. The mother may board the child, paying the board from her own earnings or with the assistance of the child's father or of relatives. The difficulties she frequently encounters in finding the right kind of boarding house and in seeing that adequate care is given are serious. Often the mother is lacking in intelligence, is financially unable to meet her responsibilities, or is careless as to the child's welfare, paying board irregularly and seldom visiting the home.

5. The child may be adopted or taken permanently by relatives or foster parents and brought up as their own child. If the foster home is a favorable one and the child not difficult to control, conditions of normal family life may be approximated.

6. The child may be taken over by a child-caring agency and placed in a boarding or free home under conditions as nearly normal as possible.

Each one of these adjustments has been tried thousands of times by those having to deal with the problem.

In planning for the future of the unmarried mother who is desirous of keeping her child, several factors should be borne in mind.

1. Every case should be considered individually and no plan should be made until all the facts are available.

2. The original plan is not always the final one. It is often necessary to make several adjustments. Experience has shown that not more than 25 per cent of arrangements under the first plan tried are successful. The second plan to be tried has a greater opportunity for success, but often a third or fourth change is necessary. For instance, the original plan may provide for the girl's return with her baby to her parents' home. Financial or other reasons may require her to leave home and go to work and have her baby boarded, making a second adjustment necessary. A third change would come if she married and established a home of her own. The last-mentioned course, especially if the husband knows all of the facts in the case, is generally the most satisfactory of all. It is the solution of the problem for a majority of the unmarried mothers who have come to the writer's attention.

3. Every effort should be made to establish paternal responsibility, so as to secure financial support for the child as well as for the mother during her confinement. Many mothers who are unwilling to risk the embarrassment of the publicity of court proceedings should be willing to permit an interview with the alleged father of the child, at least. The gratifying results of suitable private approach to the man have been shown in many instances. Aside from the helpful results, accomplished by the establishment of paternity and the obtaining of financial support for the child, contact with the man is advisable from the standpoint of social investigations. An interview with the man named by a girl as the father of her child has sometimes been most helpful in planning for the future of the mother and the child.

The Children's Bureau of the United States Department of Labor has recently concluded an interesting study of children of illegitimate birth whose mothers have kept their custody.[1] The cases of 253 children, all of whom were 8 years of age or older, were included. The histories were supplied by 27 organizations in 11 cities. Every one of the adjustments suggested in this chapter were used by the mothers in question and the results shown from actual case records. The following conclusions are drawn from the study:

1. The place in the community of the children included in the study may be regarded as similar in many respects to that of children of legitimate birth.

2. At the time of the last information a considerable proportion of the children were members of family groups sharing normal home life.

3. Although it is recognized that there are cases in which a child of illegitimate birth may not be provided for adequately by his own people the presumption is in favor of placing him with them wherever possible. No child should be committed to the care of any one not a relative until it is absolutely certain that such a course is necessary and that the child's interests demand it.

4. In a large proportion of the cases the number of changes in environment and care was not great; and it was shown that such changes as were necessary were usually made with the advice and assistance of the organization that assisted the mother in her first adjustment.

The report concluded with the following recommendations:

1. Affiliation of maternity homes with child agencies in order that provision may be made for the supervision of children when they are discharged from a maternity home.

[1] "Children of Illegitimate Birth Whose Mothers Have Kept Their Custody." U. S. Department of Labor, 1929.

2. Provision by social agencies for temporary care in boarding houses or other institutions for unmarried mothers and their children, who are not readily adjusted in the homes of relatives, in their places of employment, or in other family homes.

3. Greater willingness on the part of both public and private agencies to aid unmarried mothers in caring for their children.

4. More intensive attempts by social agencies to establish paternity in order that part at least of the support of children of illegitimate birth may be obtained from their fathers.

CHAPTER SEVEN

ORGANIZATION AND OPERATION OF AGENCIES TO ASSIST THE UNMARRIED MOTHER

Study of the Field. A careful and exhaustive study of the field should be made before any attempt is made to start a new agency or extend the activities of existing agencies. Consultation should be had with State and city officials, heads of institutions dealing with the unmarried mother and child-welfare agencies, directors of community chests or other similar organizations, social service workers, clergymen, physicians, and other persons who are in touch with the situation. The number of illegitimate births during the year, the type of service rendered by agencies already established, the attitude of hospitals toward performing the necessary obstetrical work for a maternity home which has no hospital facilities, and the financial support that can reasonably be expected, all have an important bearing on the subject.

After a survey has been made by those locally interested, it is generally advisable to secure the services of an outside expert to study the data already secured and prepare a final report. Several national organizations are prepared to furnish this expert service at nominal cost. The National Florence Crittenton Mission, for instance, so far as its resources permit, makes such surveys without cost to the local communities.

Types of Agencies. The types of agencies that can render effective aid to the unmarried mother and her child include the following:

THE CARE OF THE UNMARRIED MOTHER

1. Groups organized in small towns or suburbs of large cities who give assistance to cases originating in their own communities. Knowledge of girls needing help is brought to their attention by charitable organizations, physicians, clergymen, and other societies. The unmarried mother is generally sent to a maternity home or hospital in a large city with which the local group has some sort of affiliation. If the girl has no financial resources the local group assists in paying her expenses in the institution to which she is sent. If she returns home upon her discharge from the institution, she is assisted in reestablishing herself, employment is often found, and financial and other help is given to permit her to retain custody of her baby. The value of such service rendered to an unmarried mother by a group of sympathetic women can not be calculated. It is a type of service that has grown rapidly in recent years. The Florence Crittenton League of Compassion in Boston has 18 groups of this character, with a membership of 3,000; the Washington, D. C., Florence Crittenton Home has 20, with a membership of 2,000; and a large number of other maternity homes have similar affiliations.

2. Temporary shelters or homes for girls and children until they can be transferred to a more suitable institution or otherwise placed. This type of institution, of which there are some 100 in the United States, is generally housed in a small residence, and has accommodation for 10 to 20 girls and children. It is generally in the charge of a matron or house mother. As a rule it has no hospital facilities and no special training is given to the inmates. Girls remain for periods of several days to as many months. These institutions have considerable value, and many of the present maternity homes which are doing a more extended service commenced their work as temporary homes.

3. Maternity homes which give prenatal confinement and postnatal care of the mother, care for the baby, training for the girl, and supervision for the mother and child after they leave the home. Maternity homes may or may not have hospital facilities for the actual confinement. In more than half of the maternity homes in the United States this service is rendered. In others the obstetrical work is done in a hospital with which the home has some sort of affiliation. There is much to be said both for and against the giving of medical care in the home. Some authorities maintain that it is more costly for the community to supply proper equipment and service for physical and obstetrical examinations, and also for confinement care; others feel that it is much better to give all the care in the home, whatever the cost. It is claimed that the unmarried mother especially is less likely to be a further expense to society if her care is given under the influence of the home, particularly the bedside care. There is a difference in the extent of the follow-up work performed by maternity homes. Some have staffs of paid workers who study the girls during their stay in the home, assist them in planning for the future, and keep track of them after they have been discharged. Others depend upon volunteer workers who perform the same functions; while still others turn over all of their follow-up work to child-welfare agencies or other organizations that specialize in this form of endeavor. Some maternity homes have a boarding department where babies of unmarried mothers may be boarded by the mother after she has left the institution.

4. Child-welfare or similar organizations which assist all children whether born in or out of wedlock. Agencies of this character are located practically in every city of the United

States and do a valuable work for the child and incidentally for the mother. Some of these have boarding homes where children are boarded for mothers while at work; others have day nurseries where children may be left during the day.

Conclusion. It is the opinion of the writer that the most effective service to the unmarried mother of normal mentality and who is under 25 years of age can be rendered by maternity homes having their own hospital facilities for prenatal, confinement and postnatal care, and with a paid social worker to make investigations and do follow-up work in connection with other welfare agencies. Such homes should not be established in cities of less than 50,000 population. The remainder of this chapter is devoted to a consideration of methods that will lead to the establishment of such institutions and the improvement of the technique of existing institutions.

Character of Work of Maternity Homes. After it is determined that a maternity home of the character described above is necessary, three factors remain to be decided:

1. Shall the home have its own hospital department for confinements or shall these take place in a hospital with which arrangements can be made for this service? It might be pointed out in addition to what has already been said that as every maternity home must have a trained nurse to give prenatal and postnatal care of the mothers and care for the babies, as well as to assist in the training of the girls, especially those who desire to take courses in nursing, the confinement problem is not as complicated as is generally considered.

2. Shall girls with venereal diseases be admitted? Upon the decision of this point will depend the necessity of providing places for their isolation and treatment. The provision for

girls who have venereal diseases is not a problem as great as is generally considered. A fuller discussion will be found on pages 139 and 151.

3. Shall the home admit both white and negro girls? In the South care for both races in the same institution is manifestly impossible. In the East, North, and West, it presents special problems that must be given consideration.

4. Shall the home have a department for boarding babies? Some homes board babies until they are two years old, while others keep babies until they are six years old.

While some of these features may be developed and changes made in the original plans as the work develops, it is well to give them consideration at the beginning especially if a new plant is to be erected.

Legal Organization. Every maternity home should be incorporated under the laws of the State in which it is established. In many States the laws require incorporation in order to hold property; but whether or not it is compulsory, it is desirable. To engage in the work of caring for unmarried mothers and their children is to assume a most serious responsibility and should therefore be permitted only to those who are definitely organized for the purpose, who are of suitable character, and who possess or have reasonable assurance of securing the funds needed for their purpose.

Governing Board. The governing board should be elected by a vote of the supporting members directly or by a representative body. At present governing boards originate in three ways:

(a) Election by membership group.
(b) Appointment by governing body such as church conference, national organigation, or lodge council.

(c) Selection of new members by the board, which thus becomes self-perpetuating.

The first two methods are in accord with democratic principles; but the third method is not, and should not be abandoned when possible. In an endowed institution the board is usually self-perpetuating.

The members of the board should be representative of the supporting membership and of the territory in which the organization functions. Every maternity home should include on its board, if possible, a physician, a clergyman, a lawyer, a teacher, and a housekeeper. Parents are particularly desirable. There should be both men and women on the board.

Executive and Other Committees. When the governing board is larger than 9 to 12 members, thus becoming an unwieldy body for discussion and working out of business details, an executive committee of 3 to 5 members is essential. The officers of the board should be ex-officio members of the executive committee. The board should be divided into several active committees such as finance, building, house, admissions and dismissals, religious, legal, entertainment, and after-care committees. The chairman of the finance, house, and admission and dismissal committees should, if possible, be on the executive committee.

Meetings of Boards and Committees. The governing board should meet at least monthly. These meetings should, if possible, be held at the home where a luncheon for the board members could be provided. The executive committee should meet more often. The admission and dismissal committee should be prepared to meet at any time when called by the president or superintendent.

Duties. Each member of the board should attend all board meetings, visit the institution frequently, and make such studies as will aid him in making decisions wisely. Board members should study the methods by which similar institutions are conducted and also the relation of their work to the welfare of the community, the county, and the State. They should attend conferences dealing with illegitimacy and other child-welfare problems. They should put the development of mothers and babies ahead of financial and other considerations in the affairs of the institution.

The board is responsible to the public for the general policies of the institution. The board employs without term the superintendent and is responsible to the public for the conduct of the institution. The board is directly charged with matters relating to the purchase of the plant, erection of buildings, and securing of equipment, and with the collection and supervision of the disbursement of funds (including provision for an annual audit of accounts). The legal and moral obligations of the board may be summarized as follows:[1]

In general, the legal obligations of the board include the faithful and economical handling of funds, the careful conservation of the health, morals and education of those under its care, and the conscientious execution, as far as possible, of the benevolent intention of the founders.

The moral obligation of the trustees is broader than the legal obligation. It demands that the trustees shall qualify for their responsibility by careful individual study of the institution and by observation of the organization and administration of other similar institutions.

The moral obligation of a board of trustees is not restricted to the inmates only. It extends to the homes and relatives from whom they come. It extends also to the employees of the institution. It is a part of their duty not only to select faithful and conscientious people, but to see to it that they receive such

---

[1] Hart, Hastings H.: "The Job of being a Trustee," pp. 4, 5. Russell Sage Foundation Monograph No. 1, New York, 1915.

compensation and have provided for them such opportunities and such living conditions as to enable them to discharge properly the duties for which they are employed.

The board or executive committee should work out policies and plans in meetings with the superintendent. They should delegate to the superintendent the full responsibility for the execution of the plans and details of administration (except raising funds and equipping the plant).

The superintendent is directly responsible to the board or executive committee, not to individual members of the board nor to other committees. After her plans have been approved by the board, she should be allowed to carry them out as long as she is found competent.

Any criticisms of the superintendent or suggestions for change in her policies should be brought before the executive committee with the superintendent present. When a decision has been reached the superintendent should be willing to put the will of the board into effect. If she is unwilling to do so, she must be replaced by another superintendent. The morale of an institution may be destroyed and a competent superintendent forced to resign because board members, officers, or committeemen usurp her power, or are guilty of unwarranted meddling. Through the superintendent's reports to the board, frequent visits of board members to the institution, and the cooperation of members and special committees with the superintendent, the quality and competency of the superintendent may be ascertained and needed changes in administration may then be brought to the attention of the executive committee. Commenting upon the relationship between the superintendent and the board, Dr. Kate Waller Barrett said:

Apparently one of the most difficult things to adjust is the relative authority of the board and the superintendent. It is seldom that more or less friction is not engendered upon this point, and yet there is absolutely no necessity that it should be so. A board has no right to put a woman in charge of girls, for whom they are responsible, in whose character they have not the most implicit confidence. While she may occasionally make mistakes in dealing with the questions that arise, if she is the right kind of a woman, the mistakes will be of such a character that they do not reflect upon her integrity of purpose. There is no position of which I know that requires so many qualifications as that of superintendent, and none that necessitates more thorough abnegation of self. While the opportunities that present themselves for doing good are practically limitless, they are of such character that they do not appeal to any one unless the whole heart is in the work.

One may have every material facility for a successful institution, the board may be all that a board can be, and yet if the superintendent does not possess that wise discernment of character, coupled with Christ-like patience and sympathetic firmness, the work is sure to be a failure.

Where differences which are questions of principle arise between the superintendent and board, and neither side can give up without compromising themselves, it is always the wiser plan for the superintendent to withdraw. There is no use for her to try to combat the fixed principles of the board. If there is no harmony between the superintendent and board, the work in the home is sure to suffer, and she herself placed at a great disadvantage. Therefore, while she may feel that she is in the right, in order to do her work she should find a position where the sentiment in the board under which she works will be more in accordance with her own ideas.

The Staff. The staff for a maternity home, to do effective work, should consist of a minimum of three persons, a superintendent, a matron or housekeeper, and a trained nurse. In the small institution the first two of these offices can be held by one person and in some instances the superintendent also fills the position of trained nurse, but in no event should there be less than two paid employees. In addition to the staff of three, a paid social service worker to do investigating and follow-up work should be employed whenever it is possible. This staff will take care of the needs of an institution with from 20 to 40 girls and 15 to 30 babies. For a larger number of girls it will be necessary to have an assistant nurse or matron for each additional 10 or 15 girls. For larger institutions a teacher and recreation supervisor is desirable. Larger institutions may also find an executive secretary to handle the finances and correspondence necessary.

As the writer is convinced that the best results are obtained in maternity homes caring for from 25 to 35 girls, rather than larger institutions, he feels that the minimum of three, with an outside worker wherever possible, is the most satisfactory number on a staff.

Executive Head (*Superintendent*). The woman chosen to direct a maternity home should be well educated. Experience in general social work is very desirable. She should possess executive ability and be energetic and resourceful, and her character should be above reproach. She should have some knowledge of either nursing or domestic science in order to supervise the training of girls in these branches. She should be sympathetic by nature so as to view the girl and her problem with an understanding heart. For Christian institutions, superintendents should have a firm conviction in the power of Jesus Christ to redeem. Harsh and austere women, especially those who have been employed in penal and state reformatories for girls, do not make good superintendents of maternity homes. Dr. Kate Waller Barrett summed up the requirements of a superintendent as follows:

The first requirement is that she can absolutely forget the past of those under her charge, and that she is able to disassociate entirely in her mind that one particular sin, from which they are suffering, from the other different faults which we are trying to help them overcome. Unless a woman can rise superior to the social code, and in her heart and mind, as well as in her words, forget the fact that a girl has placed herself under a social ban, she has no right to place herself in a position where she will come in contact with such. Her very personality will be like a miasma in the atmosphere, debilitating or frustrating every new-born ambition. Every tender bud of aspiration needs an atmosphere of genial love in which to fructify, and this atmosphere, in a maternity home, is made largely by the superintendent's attitude.

Therefore, the other necessary qualifications of a superintendent must be built upon this foundation—the God-given, God-like quality of forgetfulness of everything except the present moral attitude of her charges. I need not add to this requirement that the superintendnt should b a Christian, for unless she is a child of God, she can never have this gift of forgetfulness. It is learned only in the shadow of the Cross.

We have said that the first word in the superintendent's vocabulary is "Love"; the second is "Obedience." Unless she herself has the spirit of obedience towards the board and the rules they make, we cannot hope for anything but shallow eye-service on the part of the girls.

The next word is "Teach." We would recommend the 119th Psalm as a good sermon on this subject. A superintendent who does everything herself, who does not depend upon her subordinates, and fails to teach the girls to do things, is almost as bad as one who does nothing.

A superintendent who had been accused of being distant in her manner upon first acquaintanceship, once said to me: "I would rather have the girls love me when they go away than when they first come." There was a world of good sense in that remark, and it gave me food for thought. How often is it that one may love a person when they first see them because of their affable, pleasant way, but after a short acquaintance, the "cloven foot" is displayed, and we see certain traits and lack of character that make us feel that we would not care for the friendship and advice of that person.

A superintendent might not have the qualities to win the girls when they first enter the home, and yet if she can retain their respect and their belief in her wisdom and impartiality when they leave the home, they will look to her as a wise advisor and counsellor. They will be more apt to keep in touch with her, and they will come to her to solve the difficulties that will arise in their lives.

God has not vouchsafed to all of us the personality that wins love, but He has given us an opportunity to deserve the respect of everybody with whom we come in contact. It is not necessary that we have the love of people in order to help them, but it is absolutely necessary that we have their respect. Therefore, in all our dealings, our aim should be to act in such a way that it will entitle us to the respect rather than the love of those with whom we come in contact.

Superintendents are neither born nor made. They are the products of both gifts and graces. It does not matter how well equipped mentally and physically she may have come into this world, or how good her natural temperament may be, she will also need the grace of God which comes only from a personal experience, specific training, and experience before she can do her best work.

The superintendent should plan and direct, with the cooperation of the board, all affairs of the institution, except the raising of its funds. Her duties include especially the following:

(a) Responsibility for buying all supplies.

(b) Attending meetings of the board and submitting regular written reports of her work. This report should be followed by a discussion of the details of her policies so that there may be a complete understanding and agreement on the plans and purposes of the administration by the board and the superintendent.

(c) Assisting the board to understand the social problems involved in the admission, discharge, and training of girls.

(d) Employing the other members of the staff and assuming responsibility for their work.

(e) Studying the needs of the girls in the institution and learning through conferences, visits, and study, the most progressive method of caring for them.

(f) Providing for frequent personal conferences with members of the staff and with the girls; seeking to create a spirit of cheerfulness and good fellowship and mutual trust.

(g) Providing educational and recreational facilities for the staff, at least one full day a week of relief from duty, and at least two weeks' annual vacation with pay.

(h) Attending meetings of the social workers in the community in which the home is located.

(i) Keeping records of admissions and dismissals, births, and other records required by the board.

(j) Interviewing all parents and friends of girls desiring to enter the home, as well as the girl herself, and concluding all financial arrangements after the terms have been agreed upon by the board or the proper committee.

(k) Personally censoring all mail in case it is the policy of the institution to censor the mail of inmates.

(l) Giving religious and educational training to the girls when arrangements have not been made for it to be done otherwise.

(m) Planning for the recreation of the girls in cooperation with the committee on recreation.

In addition she may be called upon to present accounts of the work before societies, church organizations, lodges, etc., and attend sessions of the committees of the community chest or similar organizations supporting the institution. If the home belongs to a national organization she should attend the annual conferences or conventions of such organizations, and her expenses to such meetings should be paid by the board.

The Matron or Housekeeper. The matron or housekeeper should be in charge of all of the domestic arrangements of the home and assist in the training of the girls in cooking, laundering, etc. Her duties include especially the following:

(a) The supervision of the preparation of food; the suggestion, after consultation with the superintendent and nurse, of menus suitable for the inmates; charge of the pantry; the keeping track of supplies and timely advice to the superintendent of the requirements of the home; the purchase of food and other supplies when delegated by the superintendent to look after them.

(b) Supervision of the laundry; responsibility for the care of clothing, laundry supplies, etc.

(c) Supervision of all housecleaning, window washing, floor polishing, etc.

(d) Supervision of the furnace room in the event a furnace man is not employed; keeping track of fuel, etc.

(e) Supervision of the grounds; responsibility for keeping them in order in case a gardener is not employed.

(f) Joint supervision with the superintendent and nurse of the girls during their recreation and rest periods.

(g) Assignment of girls placed under her charge by the superintendent to definite tasks and training them in cooking, laundering, sewing, housekeeping, etc.

(h) Supervision of the sewing room and responsibility for all materials, supplies, etc.

(i) Assignment of bath hours to inmates and responsibility for maintenance of schedule.

The Nurse. The nurse should be a graduate nurse. In small institutions where the obstetrical work is done in outside hospitals a practical nurse can be employed, but most of the State regulations for maternity homes require the employment of a graduate nurse. Her specific duties are as follows:

(a) To have charge of all the hospital work of the institution, including prenatal, confinement, and postnatal care of the girls.

(b) To have charge of the nursery and care of the babies.

(c) To have charge of the physical examination of all applicants for admission.

(d) To make examination of all inmates at regular periods for special physical defects, such as diseased tonsils, adenoids, dental defects, eye-strain, and to make recommendation for such special surgical or other treatment as is required.

(e) To instruct the girls in personal hygiene and the care of babies.

(f) To conduct nursing classes for the girls who desire to become trained nurses, practical nurses, midwives, and baby nurses.

(g) To keep physical records of each girl and baby in the institution.

Social Worker. The social worker should be a woman who has had special training in social investigation and case work. Good judgment and tact are essential for this purpose. Her specific duties are as follows:

(a) To make an investigation of the facts surrounding each applicant for admission.

(b) To keep in touch with the families or friends of the girls in the home.

(c) To study the girls while they are in the home so as to intelligently recommend plans for their future.

(d) To be responsible for all court work which is necessary to establish the paternity of babies or secure support from putative fathers.

(e) To keep complete case records of all inmates.

(f) To recommend plans for the future of the mother and child.

(g) To assist girls in securing employment and in finding suitable boarding places for them and their babies.

(h) To keep in touch with girls and their children after they leave the institution, either by correspondence or personal visits; to interest other organizations or groups in helping and encouraging unmarried mothers and their children.

(i) To attend meetings of social workers and keep in touch with other organizations interested in mother and child-welfare problems.

CHAPTER EIGHT

THE PLANT OF A MATERNITY HOME

Importance of Suitable Plant. The importance of a suitable plant for a maternity home can not be overestimated. Much of the criticism of maternity homes has been due to the lack of facilities provided in the obsolete buildings used. Old, unsuitable, and unsanitary buildings, located in the slums of big cities, are discouraging to workers and inmates alike. It is no wonder that girls refuse to remain in such places for the time that is necessary for them to receive training that is desirable. On the other hand, modernly equipped buildings which are homelike and attractive are an inspiration to those who live within their walls. The writer has known of maternity homes that were completely transformed by being moved into new buildings. In the old building, which was dark, crowded, and unsanitary, the work was most difficult. Friends and visitors, as well as board members, were discouraged by the dismal surroundings. Girls were unwilling to stay the specified time. It was impossible to give them proper recreation and training. Babies did not thrive because of lack of sun and air. The cost of repairs and maintenance was a severe drain upon the finances of the institution. When the new building in the suburbs was occupied an entire new spirit was apparent. Board members delighted to bring their friends to see the work in which they were interested. The girls were contented, and there was no difficulty in getting them to stay. There were opportunities for wholesome outdoor as well as indoor recreation. The babies had an abundance of sun and air and thrived prodigously. The cost of repairs was negligible, and maintenance expenses greatly reduced.

Location. The location of a maternity home should, if possible, be in the suburbs of a city of more than 50,000 inhabitants. The following factors enter into the selection of the site:

(a) Sufficient area to provide plenty of space for light and air around the building and to have enclosed side or back yards for recreation and domestic purposes.

(b) Easy access to a trolley or bus line and proximity to paved automobile road, so that the institution can be reached easily by physicians, relatives, and friends, and be within a reasonable distance of recreation and entertainment for the inmates and staff.

(c) Proximity to a city equipped with ample fire-fighting apparatus.

(d) Assurance of abundant supply of pure water; adequate drainage and sewerage connection.

(e) Access to primary and secondary public schools in the event that it is desirable to send young girls to such institutions.

Size of Lot and Plot Plan. It is as great a mistake to have too large a lot as to have one that is too small. For the institution caring for 25 to 40 girls a plot of ground 100 by 200 feet will be sufficient. Some institutions have much larger plots and keep cows and chickens, and plant a garden for their own needs, but as a rule these plans have not worked out very satisfactorily. The building should, if possible, be located near the street. While front yards are attractive and add to the appearance of the building, they are costly to maintain and are rarely used by the girls and children. On the other hand, large back yards are especially desirable. These should be enclosed with a high wooden fence to assure privacy. A portion of the back yard should be used for domestic purposes, but ample space should be provided for recreation facilities. Basket-ball and tennis courts, croquet grounds, and swings provide means for outside recreation that is extremely desirable during the spring, summer, and fall.

Buildings. The type of building will largely depend upon the character of work to be undertaken and the financial resources at hand. Very often it is necessary to start a home in a remodeled residence, and practically every maternity home in the country was first housed in a building of that character. When it is necessary to use a building already constructed, the following factors should be given consideration:

(a) The location of the building on the lot should be such that plenty of air and light are given on all sides.

(b) The lot should be sufficiently large to provide for additions on the rear or side, and to have space in the back for recreation and domestic purposes.

(c) The building should be of brick or cement construction with slate or metal roof so that the fire risk as well as maintenance costs are minimized.

(d) The building should be capable of being easily remodeled to meet the needs of the institution, especially by the addition of sleeping porches and sun parlors for the girls and babies.

(e) The heating plant and sanitary facilities should be sufficient to meet the needs of the institution.

In reference to remodeled buildings, Dr. Barrett once said:

Usually in the selection of a house we have to be guided more by our purse than by the fitness of the building and its surroundings for a maternity home; but even a poorly planned house, judiciously arranged, can have the home features which may be lacking in a building planned and built for the especial purpose of a home. In the latter a great many institutional features are apt to creep in, which can never be overcome by any internal ornamentation. For my own part, I would prefer a big, old-fashioned, roomy house in a quiet part of the city; a house that could be remodeled to give the necessary apartments and conveniences, and yet one which breathes "home" from every angle.

New Building. When a new building is planned, it is desirable to select a competent architect and leave all technical matters to him. The architect should be experienced in hospital or institutional construction, and should visit one or more maternity homes which have a modern plant in order to familiarize himself with their special facilities.

The following should be given consideration in planning new buldings:

Simplicity, safety, and durability are the chief factors to be considered in outside construction.

Facility in maintaining sanitary conditions should be one of the guiding principles.

Exterior wall surfaces should conform to general local practice in dwelling-house construction, except that in two-story buildings the walls should invariably be so constructed as to prevent rapid spread of fire (this applies also to all partitions).

Outside construction and surfaces should be simple and durable so that upkeep costs may be kept as low as possible.

The old-fashioned guillotine double-hung windows are most reliable and satisfactory.

No baseboards should be used unless they can be so constructed as to obviate crevices in which vermin may hide.

Floors in living rooms, dining rooms, and dormitories should be of hardwood—maple, oak, or long-leaf yellow pine—ripsawed. If concrete construction has been used, a linoleum covering is advisable. Tile, terrazzo, cement, mastic, or linoleum will be serviceable for floors of kitchens, pantries, laundries, and back entrances.

Since bathrooms, wash rooms, and toilets need to be cleaned daily, and the dining room and kitchen need to be cleaned at least three times a week, their floors should be of a material which can be scrubbed or cleaned easily. Battleship linoleum or composite floors are especially recommended for these.

On walls and ceiling a hard plaster should be used. It is advisable to use cement plaster to a height of four feet on the walls. The ceilings of basements should be made fireproof.

Fire escapes are needed in all buildings higher than two stories; and there should be at least two exits from all second stories. These must be so arranged that the inmates can escape from any part of the building and from any room. They should be so arranged that the inmates need not pass by windows on the way down. Fire escapes should be of a type to comply with the city or State building code. Chemical fire extinguishers should be placed in all halls.

All doors should open outward, and all outside doors should be equipped with automatic fire locks.

Lavatory, bath, and toilet facilities must be adequate and sanitary. These rooms should be so placed as to receive direct sunlight at some period of the day because of the value of sunlight as a disinfectant.

Cheap plumbing should be avoided. It is expensive in the end and usually causes unsanitary conditions. One bowl with running hot and cold water to four girls, and one tub or shower to six or eight girls, each in a separate compartment, should be provided.

One toilet to six to eight girls should be provided. Each toilet should be in a separate compartment, not only to inculcate modesty but also to avoid any moral hazard. Porcelain sinks should be placed on each floor, so as to be available for scrubbing and cleaning purposes.

Screens are needed on all windows, doors, and ventilators. A 16-mesh wire screen protects against mosquitoes as well as flies.

The building should be heated by a central heating plant using either hot-water or steam heat. As it is not always convenient or desirable to employ a furnace man, and the heating plant is generally operated by the girls, the use of oil as a fuel is recommended. Open fireplaces are desirable in the girls' sitting-rooms.

Sleeping porches should be provided for both the girls and the babies. These should preferably be enclosed with guillotine double-hung windows, and heated so as to be used as a work or recreation room during the day. However, they may be open and screened. The porches should be so located as to receive a maximum of sun.

Provision should be made for a well-lighted and ventilated laundry with drying room attached. The laundry should be equipped with stationary tubs, washing machines, and electric irons, rather than large laundry equipment such as mangles, ironing machines, etc., in order that the girls may be trained to use the laundry equipment which they will find in the ordinary home in which they may live or be employed after leaving the institution.

The size of the dormitories or sleeping rooms for the girls needs special consideration. Some institutions use single rooms, others rooms for two girls, while still others use large dormitories accommodating eight to twenty girls each. It is the opinion of the writer that the best results are obtained in having sleeping rooms of different capacities. For instance, in a home for thirty girls there should be three rooms for one girl each, six rooms for three girls each, and two rooms for five girls each. With this elasticity, it is possible to group girls so far as their sleeping arrangements are concerned according to age, character, educational qualifications, etc. In discussing this question, Dr. Barrett said:

We are frequently asked which we have found more suitable, single bed-rooms or the dormitory plan. If I should be guided by the experience of past years, and were at liberty to plan a house for a maternity home, I should certainly have the majority of the rooms large enough to accommodate three persons, each person to be provided with her own toilet articles and a folding screen, to insure proper privacy.

In addition to these rooms, I would also have some single bed-rooms. The reason for this opinion on my part is, that after having dealt with many thousands of girls, and having given the single-room system a thorough trial, I have found that a large number of girls who come to us are not benefited by being placed in a room alone. To rescue workers, I need not enlarge on this point. But apart from any abnormal tendency which may exist, many of our girls are low-spirited, especially when they first come to us, and are inclined to be moody in their temperaments, and it is better that they have wholesome society. If two girls are put together in a room, often unwise friendships are formed, and the family is apt to be broken up into pairs or cliques. The old adage, "Two is company, but three is a crowd," proves true in this case; the third one in the room forming a kind of balance wheel for the other two.

Ample closet and storage space should be provided. A storage room is necessary for the girls' trunks, traveling bags, extra clothing, bedding, etc. The storeroom for food supplies and extra household supplies should be sufficiently large so that wholesale quantities can be purchased and stored. Adequate refrigeration is important and an automatic refrigerating plant is suggested as economical and convenient. A small refrigerator is required in the diet kitchen. Closets for linen are necessary on the hospital and bedroom floors. Provision must be made for brooms, and other cleaning apparatus on each floor. Closets for medicines and hospital supplies should be located near the delivery room and hospital ward. In the nursery, or room adjoining, there should be cupboards or drawers for the clothing of the babies. Closets are not recommended in bedrooms or dormitories, but in their place steel lockers should be provided for each girl. These can be placed either in the sleeping rooms or in separate locker rooms conveniently located.

The delivery room should be large enough to permit efficient obstetrical work. It should have a maximum of artificial and natural light. The floor should be covered with linoleum. Space should be provided for the sterilizing apparatus, cabinet for instruments, medicines and surgical supplies. It should contain a lavatory with hot and cold water.

The hospital ward should be located near the delivery room. In a home for 25 to 35 girls, it should have accommodations for four girls. It should be well lighted and ventilated. The floor should be covered with linoleum. Two or three single bedrooms adjoining the hospital ward should be provided for girls who are very ill. One of these may be used as a rest room by the physician when waiting. Every hospital ward should be provided with a scale for the weighing of the babies.

A diet kitchen is necessary and should be conveniently placed to the hospital ward and nursery. Its equipment should consist of a sink with hot and cold running water, a small gas stove, and a refrigerator.

The rooms for the daytime activities should be large enough to accommodate comfortably the group for whom they are intended. The girls' sitting-room should be of sufficient size so that all of the girls can be accommodated there at one time. Sewing-room and classrooms are essential. Reception-rooms for the public must be ample. It should be borne in mind that in a home for 30 girls, a third or even a half of this number may have visitors at one time on visitors' days.

A Model Building. A building in which practically all of these features have been incorporated was constructed in 1927 by the Florence Crittenton Home of Seattle, Washington. It represents a maximum of efficiency at a low cost. A description of its main features may be valuable.

The building is located on the outskirts of the city on a hill with a delightful outlook. It is two and one-half stories high, 37 by 100 feet in size, with a flat specification room. The walls from the foundation to the first floor are concrete and above that brick. Ordinary red common brick were used, but for the outside course they were hand-picked. Cut-stone window sills and a cut-stone coping add to the appearance.

There are two stairways, one at each end of the building, both constructed of concrete and enclosed in fire-proof walls.

On the first or basement floor are located the dining-room with accommodations for 40 persons, the pantry, the kitchen, the food storerooms, the laundry, the drying-room, the furnace-room, a storage-room for trunks, bedding, and clothing, and

NEW BUILDING OF FLORENCE CRITTENTON HOME, SEATTLE, WASH.

two isolation-rooms. Toilets are provided for the girls working on this floor and separate toilet and shower for the isolation-rooms. On the main floor are located the office, the reception-room, the superintendent and nurse's room, with bath between, the delivery room, the hospital ward, the diet kitchen, three private bedrooms, the nursery, and a large sun parlor, 25 by 35 feet in size, for the babies.

On the top floor, at each end of the building, is located a large room, 25 by 35 feet in size. One of these is the girls' sitting-room, and the other the girls' workroom. The latter is steam-heated, but has windows on all sides so that it is easily converted into a sleeping porch and used for that purpose in the summer months. The balance of the top floor is divided into sleeping-rooms for one, three, or five girls each, and accommodates 24 girls. A locker-room is provided. Stairways lead to the roof, which is used for recreation purposes.

Cost of Seattle Building. The cost of the Seattle building was $35,000, but this cost is regarded as exceptionally low. In the average community of the United States a building of this size and character will cost from $40,000 to $50,000. If the building is fireproof the cost will be from $70,000 to $80,000.

Furnishings. The rooms in an institution should not differ greatly from similar rooms in a comfortable private residence. A homelike effect must be sought. The choice of colors for walls should be made carefully. Cheerful colors rarely cost any more than depressing ones, and the atmosphere of a room depends largely upon the background furnished by its walls. Pretty window draperies should be used. Materials of good quality are cheaper in the end than those which cost little at the start but need to be replaced soon. Dr. Barrett's ideas on this subject are interesting. She said:

In our home we do not put all the prettiest furniture in the parlor, leaving the broken and unsightly objects for the bedrooms of the girls. It does not matter how simple the furnishings may be, if they are only whole and clean they have a beauty of their own. We try to have our house grow prettier the farther we get from the front door. When we remember with what fastidious care we try to keep our own daughter's room the most attractive in the house and how we love to think of the purity of the furnishings as emblematic of the purity of her who occupies it, we will understand how necessary it is, when we are dealing with God's daughters, to use the same watchful care in the little details of their lives. We remember in one of our homes the matron's daughter with her own hands had shaped from unsightly boxes, by draping them in white muslin and bright cretonne, a dainty set of furniture for a room which one of the inmates was to occupy. What a profound impression it made upon the girl's mind when she entered this room! She fairly overflowed with joy. When you have made a girl's room attractive, never give yourself a little self-congratulatory pat on the shoulder and say with a tone of triumph, "It is better than she ever had before," but thank God that you have been permitted to make her life brighter and add wholesome comfort and pleasure to it. Christ has promised us a hundredfold for all we give up for His sake and the Gospel's, and we will try to give this girl the very best in our power. There will be plenty of self-denials and sorrows, as mortification of the flesh, after we have done the best to smooth the rough places in her path.

The girls' sitting-room should be particularly attractive. There should be comfortable straight chairs, rocking chairs, sofas and couches, small tables, book cases, library table, a piano, a phonograph, a radio set. Built-in seats near the fireplace are a pleasing addition. Good engravings, photographs, and prints should be hung on the wall and there should be several mirrors hung low enough to be of use. Dr. Barrett often said that their was nothing in a home that helped girls as much as looking at themselves in a mirror. An open fireplace (with screen always in place when the fire is burning) is especially desirable. On the importance of having the sitting-room attractive, Dr. Barrett said:

The best, sunniest, and brightest room should be the girls' sitting-room. If there are not two rooms, one suitable for a sitting-room and the other for a workroom, then make this big room both sitting-room and workroom. With a little care the room can be made to serve both purposes admirably. In the morning and early afternoon, it is a workroom. The tables are full of sewing materials and unfinished garments, and the sewing-machines are pulled out in conspicuous positions. When the work is done, all the instruments of toil disappear, and in their places magazines, books, and writing materials occupy the tables, and on every hand there are evidences of the social side of life.

It is most necessary that the sitting-room should be well supplied with good reading matter, the current magazines, simple books on hygiene, child study, and self-culture. Most of the girls who come to us need to be taught to love books, as very few of them have a natural fondness for reading, and in order that they may be supplied with wholesome subjects of conversation this habit of reading should be cultivated. A judicious discussion of the books and magazines on the table by the matron and the workers with the girls will do much to stimulate an interest in them. I remember on one occasion a girl who had been much given to lewd conversation was reproved for this habit by the matron. She said to her, "My dear child, aren't you ever going to stop talking about those terrible things?" The poor untrained girl burst into tears and said, "I don't know anything else to talk about."

The bedrooms should all be furnished with single, white iron beds. They should have upon them a good mattress, covered by a slip of unbleached cotton; over that a heavy pad, following which is the ordinary bedding. Blankets are usually used in the place of comforts and during the day the bed may be covered with brightly colored spreads.

The dining-room should be outfitted with sideboards, serving tables, and tables seating not more than eight girls. In some larger institutions where room is not available to have many small tables, larger tables seating more girls are used, but the small tables are best. In discussing the dining-room, Dr. Barrett said:

It is in our dining-room, possibly, that the oneness of the interests of all is most pronounced. It is a bright, sunny, English basement-room. Each table is covered with a spotless cloth, and although the table furnishings are simple, they are neat and pretty. The knives, forks, and spoons are plated silver, and a simple pattern of china is used. The tables are all furnished alike, and usually there are flowers upon each. There is a bay window to the dining-room, and in this window rests one of the tables. It seats eight, and when you look at the room you may think that this table is reserved for the officers and workers of the home; but you will be pleasantly surprised when you learn that it is reserved for the cooks and dining-room girls, whose duties prevent them from sitting at the first table. The superintendent sits at the head of one table, the matron at the head of another, and the nurse at the head of the third. Everybody eats the same sort of food and off exactly the same kind of china. The food has been prepared, cooked, and served by the girls, and is of the most wholesome and appetizing character.

We are frequently asked why we require our workers to eat at the same table with the girls. There are so many reasons for this that it would fill a book to tell them. The most important reason, of course, is that we want to be in a true sense a family, with the officers as the mother, presiding at the head of the table. It insures the girls' having good, substantial meals, because if food is not sufficient for the officers, they are pretty apt to report the same to the board, and if it is sufficient for them, of course it is for the girls.

Nursery. The following covers the principal requirements:

(a) Infant cribs or bassinettes should have firm, clean mattresses covered with rubber sheeting and washable pads. Clean woolen blankets should be used. There should be a separate bed for each infant with provision to prevent contact infection.

(b) Sanitary bathing facilities must be provided. The bathing table should be properly protected and the pad renewed after each bath. Accurate scales must be provided. Where basins are used, a separate one must be provided for each infant unless the basin is sterilized after use for each child.

(c) The temperature of the room in which the babies are bathed should be not less than 75 degrees Fahrenheit.

(d) The heating of the nursery should be sufficient to maintain a temperature of at least 70 degrees Fahrenheit in severe weather. There should be a wall thermometer hanging at the level of the crib in order to insure that an even temperature is maintained.

(e) The nursery must be an outside room, properly ventilated, and the glass area of the window space should be not less than one-fifth of the floor space. The room must be located so as to secure sunshine some portion of the day.

(f) A covered container should be provided for soiled linen.

(g) A dressing tray should be set up at all times. The following articles are recommended for dressing and caring for infants: sterile gauze, absorbent cotton, medium and small safety pins, alcohol, powdered castile soap, a proper lubricant (olive or albolene), boric acid solution, pure powder, and abdominal binder for infants.

(h) Bottles and nipples should be properly sterilized after each use.

(i) A minimum of one dozen diapers per child should be provided for each twenty-four hours. Fresh-laundered diapers only should be used.

(j) If hot water bags are used, they must be of proper temperature and covered with a flannel bag before being placed in the crib, and must not come in contact with the baby's body.

CHAPTER NINE

POLICY OF ADMISSIONS AND DISMISSALS

Policy to be Determined. A definite policy as to admissions and dismissals should be determined. The needs of the unmarried mothers in the community where the institution is organized to serve should be carefully considered. Note should be taken of all the resources of the community which are available for meeting some of the needs. Then the type of work which the institution, by virtue of its plant, staff, and financial support is best qualified to undertake, can be chosen most intelligently. The admission and dismissal policy should be reconsidered at intervals and revised when it appears that the institution can render a more valuable service.

Responsibility Should Be Definitely Fixed. The responsibility for admissions should be definitely fixed. The superintendent acting alone or in conjunction with the admission and dismissal committee of the board should control all admissions. In most maternity homes the superintendent is empowered to make decision on all emergency cases, but immediate report is made to the admission and dismissal committee for final action. The committee should meet at least weekly when there are applications to consider.

Restrictions of Admissions. The restriction of admissions involves problems of the most serious character. Factors of age, color, mentality, physical condition, delinquency, all have important bearing upon the subject. In the following discussion of these factors some points will be brought out that will assist an institution in fixing its admission policy.

Age. Restriction as to age is important. It is difficult to do good permanent work with girls and women of wide differences of age unless the home is large enough so that they can be handled in groups according to age. Women of 25 years or older have problems that are entirely different from girls of 16 or 18. As a rule they are more difficult to control, are unwilling to stay the prescribed period, and can not be trained as effectively as the younger girl. It is therefore wise to place an age limitation, and restrict the work to girls under 25 years of age. In institutions where there are more applications than can be taken care of preference should be given to still younger girls.

Color. The handling of girls of mixed races in the same institution is difficult. In the South it is practically impossible, and in the East, North, and West it presents problems that are hard to overcome. It is wise, therefore, to restrict admissions to girls of one color.

Mentality. The question of mentality is one of the most difficult to settle. Many of the unmarried mothers who apply for admission are of such low mentality that they can not be helped. Especially is this true of the feeble-minded girl. Despite increased knowledge on the subject of mental defects, there are still some individuals who maintain that a delinquent girl who is mentally defective may be trained under proper supervision. To them the cause of misconduct may seem to lie in insufficient supervision at the home, in poor educational advantages, or in some sort of faulty environment so that a change of surroundings may be capable of eradicating the defect. The history of institutional care for the feeble-minded, however, proves that a majority of these cases will show but slight improvement, even under the most ideal conditions. Feeble-minded girls and those of low mentality should only be admitted temporarily.

Physical Condition. Physical condition has an important bearing. No girl should be admitted whose physical condition will be a menace to the other inmates. For this reason it is often necessary to deny admittance to girls who are suffering with tuberculosis. As to girls who have venereal diseases there is a great difference of opinion. Most maternity homes refuse to admit girls so diseased. The writer is convinced that their attitude is not the correct one. Often the diseased girl has been infected by the same man who is responsible for her pregnancy, and she is no more to blame for her condition than the girl who has gone through a similar experience and has not been infected. The care of the venereally infected girl is not so dangerous or difficult as is generally supposed. On this point the Bureau of Public Health of the United States Government has prepared the following statement:

The Public Health Service believes not only that if proper sanitary precautions are observed there is no danger in admitting cases of venereal disease to lying-in hospitals or homes, but that the placing of such cases under proper medical care prior to confinement will, aside from the benefit extended to the expectant mothers themselves, contribute much to public welfare in general. A child born of a mother infected with gonorrhea easily may acquire an inflammation of the eyes which can and frequently does result in blindness. An infant born of a syphilitic mother is almost sure to have syphilis at birth. Proper treatment of pregnant women afflicted with venereal disease, therefore, not only will render pregnancy and confinement of less danger to the already unfortunate expectant mother, but will greatly reduce the chance of infection of the child itself before or during birth, thus eliminating both mother and child as possible sources of infection to others in the future and avoiding the possible burden of a defective upon the community.

[139]

As to the precautions necessary to protect other inmates of an institution where persons with venereal diseases are admitted, the first and most important measure recommended is the thorough examination of every patient on admission, for the detection of venereal disease if present. This examination should include laboratory tests. The "dark-field" microscopic method should be used repeatedly if necessary in determining the nature of open lesions resembling syphilis, and the Wasserman test should be made in every case.

When the diagnosis of venereal disease has been made, the patient should be put under proper treatment at once. Open lesions of syphilis can be healed in a very short time by the administration of the arsphenamines and the patient thereby rendered non-infectious to others by casual contact. A few doses of the arsphenamines, however, will not cure the disease and unless the treatment is continued for a long period of time a relapse in infectiousness may occur. Treatment should be continued as long as necessary and should be controlled carefully by laboratory tests and physical examinations. Dependence should never be placed, however, upon a single Wasserman test as an evidence of cure of syphilis. Repeated physical and laboratory examinations should be made at intervals extending over a long period of time before the patient is pronounced free of infection.

Patients with venereal disease need not be segregated. For convenience the "open" or infectious cases may be assigned to a single ward if practicable. Separate toilet facilities should be provided for the use of those with gonorrhea. Care should be taken to prevent the use by others of toilet articles used by patients with venereal disease. Although the transmission of syphilis and gonorrhea through the common use of dishes, glasses, and silverware probably is a very remote possibility, it is considered advisable to sterilize such articles after each use by a patient with venereal disease. All dressings used in the treatment of venereal infections should be handled carefully and destroyed by burning. Nurses who assist with dressings, douches, and the like, should wear rubber gloves for their own protection as well as to prevent the possible spread of infection to others.

Delinquency. The hardened delinquent girl, especially one who has been an inmate of a State reformatory, has no permanent place in a maternity home. As a rule, she dominates the younger girls and proves a real menace to them. With very young delinquents the rules should be elastic enough to provide for their admission in many cases, especially if they remain in the home for a sufficient length of time to receive the training that they require.

Residence. The place of residence of applicants for admission is a cause of constant discussion in many cities where maternity homes are located. As a rule these homes are largely supported by local charity and many of them come under the direction of community chests and similar organizations. Objection is often made to the admission of non-residents of the city or county in which the home is located. Consideration is not given, however, to the migrations of unmarried mothers. The tendency of a girl when she gets in trouble is to get as far away from home as possible. The country girl goes to the small city and the small-city girl goes to the big city. In New York City more than half the unmarried mothers in one year were from other cities. Boston girls were found in San Francisco, and California girls in Florida. Some homes solve the problem by charging a larger admission fee for non-residents.

Second Offenders. The question whether or not unmarried women in pregnancies other than the first should be admitted for care must be considered. The policy in a majority of homes is to limit assistance to unmarried women in the first pregnancy, although some institutions accept patients in later pregnancies if they had not been former patients of the institution. Some homes have felt that they have exerted every effort to assist a mother during her first residence at the institution. If they had failed, or if she has not responded, further effort on their part, they believe, would avail nothing. Others feel that having "repeaters" in the home had a decidedly bad influence on the other patients, particularly when it was known that the repeaters had been in the same institution before. On this subject Dr. Kate Waller Barrett said:

> People have frequently asked, "Would you take a girl in if she was about to become a mother the second time?" Certainly not in the majority of cases, especially if the girl's first child was born under Christian influence, and she had some one to encourage her to a better life after the first one was born. If, however, she had simply gone to a hospital and her child had been taken from her and placed in some asylum, and no one had talked to her and influenced her to a better way, I would just as leave have her under the latter condition as when her first child was born. In thinking of such cases as these, we forget how much easier it is for a woman to fall the second time than the first, how many barriers have been broken away, how much less she has to give up. Frequently a woman who has gone astray is so utterly dependent and so entirely hopeless that after spending most of my life with them, what surprises me most is that they do not fall again, or rather that they have the courage and determination to live right in the face of the cold charity that they receive at the hands of the world.

Temporary and Permanent Admissions. The board should have a policy of temporary and permanent admissions, when room and facilities make it possible. Efforts should be made to help every unmarried mother when it does not deter the development of the majority. Under a policy of temporary admissions it may be possible to give confinement care and some degree of after-care to feeble-minded girls, older women, delinquents, etc. Permanent admissions should be limited to those girls who can be definitely helped by a prolonged stay in the home.

Thorough Investigation Necessary. A thorough investigation of applications for admissions is essential to any well-conducted maternity home. This investigation need not always be made before the unmarried mother is admitted. In fact, it is best to admit her temporarily and then commence the investigation after she has been in the home a few days. Dr. Barrett's opinion on this question was as follows:

While, as a matter of record and to prevent imposition, it is necessary to have certain data in regard to each case which we admit permanently, we think it is far wiser to let the facts come out one by one, after the girl has gotten accustomed to her surroundings, and looks upon us as friends, rather than try to force them out in the first interview. Most girls when they come have prepared beforehand a pretty little story, which they have all ready to tell and which is generally lacking in the one great requisite—truth. If they are permitted to tell this story and you do not seem to believe it, you have already sown a seed of discouragement; and if you do believe it, and it is not true, then the girl has to try to live up to the character she has given herself. Frequently the remembrance of the false pretences under which she has entered the home, and to which she is too weak to confess, is the means of keeping her from making any progress in her religious life; therefore the fewer questions that are asked at first, the better. It is better to admit girls temporarily, and if, after the girl has been in the home a few days, she is found to be an unworthy object or such a case that the home can not help permanently, the only harm is that she has received a few days' board that she is not entitled to. In regard to asking her name, forbear at first, except to ask her, "What name did you love best for your mother to call you when you were a little girl at home?" Have her called by that name while she is in the home. It is a little thing, but in many cases each time she hears the name it will bring up recollections of the happy days when she was a pure-hearted girl, and thoughts of a beneficial character will be aroused.

Methods of Investigation. Some methods of accomplishing thorough investigation are as follows:

(a) The institution may employ a trained social worker to make the investigations, and this is recommended by the writer. It is important that she shall do her work in close cooperation with other social agencies in the community.

(b) Two or more small institutions may cooperate in procuring the services of a competent person. Such combinations are advisable only when the number of applications is so limited that one person can handle the joint work in an adequate manner.

(c) A private agency, such as a children's aid society or a family agency, may make investigations for an institution.

[143]

(d) A central admission agency or bureau may be maintained by a group of institutions. The group may be united by a common religious faith, or all may receive support from a common fund, or there may be a loose organization of voluntary members. Although the methods of operation in such agencies differ, time is generally saved by them for both relatives and institutional workers, duplication of work is avoided, better understanding of the children who need help is acquired, and a more satisfactory adjustment is likely to be made.

These agencies find it desirable to work very closely with the family case-work agency, for the unmarried mother's problem must be considered as a family problem and the plans made for her should include her family. When the family agency is enlisted the possibilities of adjustments in the girl's own home are greater.

The superintendent should not be expected to make the investigations. The experience and training which qualify a person for the work of superintending an institution are quite different from those required for a social case worker. Moreover, the superintendent has enough to do managing the institution, and she could not devote time to investigation without neglecting her other duties.

Volunteer workers seldom have the experience necessary to make adequate investigations or the time to devote to it. This work demands the best type of experienced social worker, just as a physician of recognized standing should be called upon for a diagnosis of the girl's physical condition.

Plans for Adjustment. No girl should be dismissed from the home until some plan has been made for her future. Some of the plans which are made practically by all homes have been discussed in previous chapters (see page 101).

It should be borne in mind that the first plan is not always the final one, and that one or more will have to be tried out until a permanent adjustment is made. On the first plan suggested—marriage to the father of the child—there should be great caution. The Children's Bureau of the United States Government makes the following comment on this subject:[1]

Many of the child-welfare boards and superintendents of maternity hospitals have not yet seen the danger of forced marriages and are allowing men to marry in order to escape imprisonment or paternity proceedings. In many instances marriage takes place after legal steps have been commenced or after the arrest of the man. The unfortunate aspect of the situation is that many times the girls fail to see that the apparent affection of the man is unreal and that their promises are being made for the sole purpose of escaping a penalty. In many cases the girl has been genuinely fond of the man, and when this is true she is more apt to relent in the prosecution, especially if he is unable to secure bail and will have to remain in jail for some months if she refuses to marry him. Then the relatives are apt to favor marriage on the traditional argument of "giving the child a name." These relatives and members of child-welfare boards would not be so hopeful of marriage as a solution of the girls' difficulties if they knew a little more about the results of forced marriage.

Length of Stay. Length of stay in a maternity home depends upon many considerations and it is difficult to fix upon any definite time limit. It will depend largely upon the size and facilities of the institution, the character of work of other agencies in the community interested in the unmarried mother and child-welfare problem, and the facts surrounding each individual case. The period may last from a few weeks in the case of the feeble-minded girl who is being given temporary care to a year or more for the young unmarried mother who requires training. As a rule, girls who can be helped permanently should become inmates of the home three months prior to their confinement and remain for at least three months after the birth of their babies. It should be the object of the maternity

---

[1] Illegitimacy as a Child-Welfare Problem," 1924, Part 3, page 223.

home to return each girl to society at the earliest possible time, taking into full consideration her health and that of her baby, her mental attitude toward life and the experiences she has just undergone, the attitude of her family and the community to which she is to return, and, if she is to earn her own living, her capabilities for so doing. As a matter of having some definite agreement with the girl and her friends, it is desirable that she sign an agreement to remain in the home for a period of at least six months.

Restrictions Upon Leaving. Even when a definite time limit as to her stay in the home has been agreed upon by the girl and her friends, many attempts will be made to have this time shortened and girls are constantly threatening to leave the home. All sorts of reasons are presented by relatives as to why the girl should be permitted to come home. Every reasonable effort should be used to combat this effort, but threats, harshness, and undue influence should be avoided. On this subject Dr. Barrett said:

There is nothing which requires more tact and patience than when we find that in spite of all our endeavors to make a girl happy and contented in the home, she is determined to leave us. Of course, we always try to impress upon the girls the fact that there is no need of running away, as the doors are always unlocked and they are never detained in the home against their wills, but we should try to reason them into staying. I say "reason" them into staying, not "persuade" them. Beware lest a little wounded vanity slip in when we find she will not consent to remain, both upon the part of the board and superintendent, which will make them feel inclined to be a little severe with the girl when she is just leaving. I can recall many a scene, the memory of which brings tears to my eyes, of just such occasions as this, when because of some untoward influence brought to bear upon some of our best girls, they had been led to leave the home. But I thank God that His grace is sufficient to make us just as gentle and tender to such an one as to the most faithful in the home, and that her last hours with us have been free from friction; that the last recollection she has carried away from the home is a warm embrace and an earnest "God bless you, my child, wherever you go." Frequently more can be done in these last few moments and in these last few words than in all the months that have gone by. Seeds have been sown which will be watered with many repentant tears, and bands of love woven which will insensibly draw her back to us again.

Admission Fees. The admission fee should be fixed by the board and collected by the superintendent. It should be a lump amount and not based on the length of stay of the girl in the home. The lump sum should include all obstetrical and other expenses and there should be no extras. No sum larger than the fixed admission fee should be collected by the superintendent and in the event of cases where the friends or relatives of the girls are able to pay a larger amount than the fixed fee they should be requested to make a donation to the institution through the treasurer and the amount of the donation may be suggested by the superintendent. The amount of the fee will depend upon local conditions, financial resources of the home, etc. In most maternity homes it ranges from $25 to $100. No girl should be refused admittance into a matrnity home operated on philanthropic principles because she can not pay the fee. In case she can not pay all or even a part, her note should be taken for the unpaid portion so as to place her on a par with all the other girls. The note will probably never be paid and in practically no instances will efforts be made to collect it, but it has a beneficial purpose. There should be no distinctions between the girl who pays the entire fee and one who pays nothing. The Philadelphia Conference on Parenthood stresses this point. It recommends:

The social treatment of maternity homes should be uniform for all mothers. Ability and inability to make adequate financial payment for the services rendered should not lead to the granting or withholding of special privileges.

THE CARE OF THE UNMARRIED MOTHER

Dr. Barrett had firm convictions on this subject. She said:

We make no difference whatever between the girl who pays us nothing and the girl who pays us $25 a month. The one is as much under our control as the other, and is expected to do her part in the work of the home just as much as the other. Sometimes her family or friends may be very foolish and not relish this treatment upon our part, but that is all the more reason we should be steadfast in our determination that the girl shall have proper training, at least while she is with us. I can best illustrate our attitude by telling a little incident that happened in our home a few years ago. A girl was brought to us by her mother, and when the mother was leaving, she did the almost un-heard-of thing of giving us a hundred dollars for the expense of the girl while she was with us. Of course this soon became noised around the home and the girls began to look upon her as a "star boarder," and she herself began to feel the importance of being one of the very small number who had anything of this world's goods. But by the time it came her turn to go into the laundry, she had gotten sufficiently into the spirit of the home not to object to doing her part in making it a home. About this time, her mother came to call upon her and I happened to be on duty. I spoke to one of the girls passing and said, "Go to the laundry and tell ———— to come to the drawing-room, her mother wishes to see her." Her mother turned around to me and said, "Do you mean to say my daughter is in the laundry?" I said, "Yes; it is her turn to assist in the house laundry this week." "But," she said, "I paid a hundred dollars for you to keep my daughter, and I did not suppose you were going to make a servant of her." I said, "We are not making a servant out of her; we are trying to make a useful woman of her." "But," she said, "my daughter never had to do any washing in her life. I always hired some one to do the rough work in my home." I turned and said: "My dear woman, if I had been so unfortunate in training my daughter that when she was 18 years old I had to bring her to a rescue home for the cause you have brought your daughter to us, I would be very glad if some one else would try a different method in dealing with her than I had tried. We can not keep your daughter, as was explained to you when you first called, unless we have the entire control of her, but if you have seen your daughter and if she says she is not happy, and if you are not satisfied that we are doing the best we can for her, you are at liberty to take her back again, and I will refund your money." Needless to say, the girl stayed and we had the reward of seeing her trained into one of the most useful girls that ever went out of our home.

CHAPTER TEN

PHYSICAL CARE

First Responsibility of Maternity Homes. The first and perhaps the most important function of a maternity home is the physical care of the mother and child, and it is the responsibility of the board and its officers to provide such facilities as will make it possible for each inmate in the home to receive the best medical service. Their obligation can be met only by—

(a) Thorough physical examination at the time of the entrance.

(b) Carrying out of the recommendations based upon examinations made (including all corrective work, the need of which is reported to be immediate).

(c) Prenatal and postnatal care according to the best standards.

(d) The best confinement care and obstetrical work either in the home itself or in a hospital.

(e) The care of the baby so that it will get the proper start in life.

The Medical and Nursing Staff. The staff for a maternity home will depend upon the size of the institution and the character of the work that is being done. Usually it should consist of one or more physicians and a nurse, with arrangements for consultation and clinic or private-office service of specialists when needed.

1. A supervising physician or head of the medical staff. In the great majority of maternity homes, especially those which have facilities for obstetrical work, the entire medical work is done by a staff of physicians who give their services to the institution without charge. The staff is elected by the board, who invite certain physicians to become members, and they in turn

elect the chief; or the board asks a physician to become the head of the medical department, and he in turn invites his associates. The staff arranges among its members the duties and times of service of the examining physician, the obstetrician, the pediatrician, the dentist, etc. In many instances each of these serve for periods of two or three consecutive months each year.

2. Examining Physician. The examining physician should make a thorough physical examination of each applicant for admission within 24 hours. This should include Wasserman tests and vaginal smears, pelvic measurements, urinalysis, and blood pressure, examination for focal infections, dental caries, or any other defect that should be treated immediately. It is preferable that the examination should be made in the home, but it can be done in the office of the examining physician. Laboratory work is done by the physician himself or at the city laboratory.

3. Obstetrician. The obstetrician in charge should make regular visits to the expectant mothers and have charge of the confinements.

4. Pediatrician. Every maternity home should have a pediatrician on the staff, who should be in charge of the babies.

5. A trained registered nurse or a practical nurse should be in residence. In many of the States, regulations of maternity homes require that the nurse be registered. In the event that the positions of superintendent and nurse are filled by the same persons, which is sometimes the case in small institutions, a visiting nurse may be called in in case of emergencies.

6. A dentist is necessary and arrangements should be made for the service in his office when required.

7. Consultation or clinic or private-office service of oculist, nose, throat and ear specialist must be sought whenever needed.

Isolation Period. All girls should be isolated for a period of two or three days before they are permitted to mingle with the other girls. Girls with venereal disease should be isolated until all danger of their infecting others is passed. Great care should be taken in permitting new girls, and especially those who are under treatment for venereal disease, to enter the nursery or handle the babies.

Medical Records. Complete medical records should be kept by the nurse in charge. In addition to the regular charts in use in all hospitals, there should be special charts for maternity work. Four of these are shown in the appendix. (See also page 190.)

Breast Feeding. The importance of breast feeding has already been pointed out in this study, and it is not necessary to go further into that subject. No single factor exercises a more pronounced influence on the development of the baby and on his health during his entire life than nursing at his mother's breast.

Treatment of Venereally Diseased Patients. (See also page 139.) Regardless of their intentions, all maternity hospitals receive at least some patients with gonorrhea and syphilis in an active stage. Such patients are received for obstetrical and not venereal disease treatment. Some hospitals, in an effort to keep out patients suffering from venereal infection, do not accept known cases. These institutions build on a false security and handle these unsuspected cases without special precautions. Even under such conditions few, if any, cross infections are known to occur. The danger would be less if venereal cases were accepted frankly and the necessary precautions taken to prevent the spread of infection. The equipment required need not be elaborate or expensive, and the technique is simple, though exact. Both are within the reach of any hospital fitted to care for maternity cases. Precautions differ in the care and treatment of syphilitic and gonorrheal cases. The syphilitic may quickly be rendered non-infectious, and such a patient, under continued treatment, is a source of practically no danger to others. The gonorrheal case is infectious throughout its course, and often requires a long period of treatment. These patients are benefited by maternity home care, and are not in need of strict hospitalization, although they frequently require bed care. Therefore, the following minimum standards relate more especially to gonorrhea:

Isolation. It is desirable, but not necessary, to provide separate quarters for infected patients. Isolations of discharges should be aimed at rather than of the individual. Successful isolation depends on methods, not separate rooms. Inexpensive equipment is required and simple technique meticulously carried out.

Treatment. It is absolutely essential that cases of venereal diseases be treated consistently and adequately during pregnancy. The treatment should be instituted as early in pregnancy as possible and carried out under competent supervision.

Equipment. Individual bed pans, jars, and basins must be provided for infected patients. Separate dishes are also advisable, but this is more important in the case of syphilis than of gonorrhea. In the latter disease, the danger of infection from this cause is so remote as to be practically negligible. Instruments, basins, and gloves used in the care of infected cases should be doubly sterilized—first, separately and then with the remaining supplies. Linen coming in direct contact with the patients must be kept separate until sterilized. The method of handling should entail no danger to the laundress.

Treatment Room. A separate treatment and examination room is not a necessity if the above precautions are followed. The patient's own bed may be used in the absence of a dressing room. The delivery room should never be used in the treatment of these cases.

Toilet and Bathing Facilities. Infected patients should never be allowed to use the toilet designated for non-infectious patients. Individual bed pans, jars, or commodes must be provided for their use. These patients should not use the tub; they should use sponge baths or showers. When shower baths are used, separate ones are not necessary for infected patients. The danger of the spread of the disease from this source is too remote.

Care of Babies. All infected infants must be isolated, but not necessarily in separate rooms. They may even be cared for in the general nursery, in which case they should be set apart from other infants by use of a screen or other means so as to prevent careless observation of technique. Isolation depends on careful technique, not on separate nurseries. It is advisable for the nurse taking care of these babies not to care for other babies, but this is not absolutely necessary. If the nurse wears gloves in handling the infants and observes known precautions, the infection will not be transmitted. Individual toilet articles and supplies must be kept for each infant. The greatest danger of spreading gonorrheal infecion to the infant of the diseased mother is from the mother's own hands. A baby must not be handled by an infected mother until such mother has been thoroughly instructed and has proved her reliability.

Psychological Examinations. The importance of having mental tests of girls who are admitted or may be admitted to maternity homes in order to plan for their future deserves serious consideration. Very little attention has been paid in the past to this study and often case records contain terms in describing mental defects which are not only inexact, but misleading. Mental tests should be made of all girls in a home by a trained psychiatrist. It is generally possible to secure the services of a psychiatrist who is either in private practice or employed in a State or municipal institution. Social workers should come, in time, to recognize not only the fairly obvious groups of mental abnormalities, but those involving a more subtle analysis.

Dr. Kammerer divides the term "mental abnormality" into five subdivisions:

1. By mental defect is meant "a definite lack of general mental ability as an irrevocable characteristic. From some cause existing in the germ plasm or occurring early in the growth of an individual, mental potentials never become normal. Full-development capacity was never present and can never be gained. Mental defect is incurable."

2. It is frequently necessary, furthermore, to recognize such groups as those which contain individuals who are mentally dull from poor physical condition, or from the indulgence in various debilitating habits.

3. Between feeble-mindedness and insanity lies psychic constitutional inferiority. Individuals belonging in this group are usually considered to be incapable of social self-control under ordinary conditions, and to be so on the border line as to prove unacceptable to either institutions for the feeble-minded or the insane.

4. Mental aberrations may occur in individuals who are not primarily mentally defective, and those who are suffering from a mental disease which is often curable as bodily diseases are curable.

5. Among those subject to some form of mental peculiarity may be included persons who cannot be said to be possessed of aberrational tendencies, but whose abnormal behavior is yet determined by some special mental twist.

Mental Abnormalities	Mental Defect	Feeble-minded	Idiot / Imbecile / Moron
		Subnormal	
		Defective only in some special ability	
	Mental Dullness from Physical Condition	Permanent / Temporary	
	Constitutional Inferiority		
	Mental Aberration (Insanities Psychoses Psychopathics)	Major Types	Chronic / Temporary
		Minor Types	Chronic / Temporary
	Mental Peculiarities		

CHAPTER ELEVEN

SPIRITUAL, MORAL AND MENTAL TRAINING

Religious Instruction. A large percentage of the girls in a maternity home are merely children so far as their knowledge of spiritual things are concerned. Many of them have had no religious instruction whatsoever, and it is necessary to commence with them almost from the beginning. Instruction in accord with the faith of their parents should be provided for all children. It should be definite and positive. Rudolph H. Reeder outlines the needs of institutional children which may be applied to girls in a maternity home as follows:

The natural starting point and the surest foundation for moral instruction is the religious instinct. Early in childhood nearly all children learn of a Supreme Being called God, and that in some way or other He is concerned in their conduct and welfare. Whether their relation to God is chiefly that of fear or love depends upon the child's early religious training. To many children, God is a being to be feared rather than loved. It has been said that man is a religious animal. At least, religious instincts seem to be basic in his nature. To permit the child to grow up, therefore, without religious training fails to develop these fundamental instincts. Early impressions persist, and it is extremely important that the child begin his religious life with impressions that draw him towards God as father, teacher, and friend whom he would like to please.

The staff must remember that upon them devolve the duties of parents as well as school-teachers. In many cases children look to them for all the religious training they will ever receive. Religious instruction should not be confined to the classroom but should be correlated with the child's daily life. Numerous opportunities are afforded the group mother during the day in the associations of the group to bring home the lessons of religion and the stories of the Bible.

It is our endeavor to make the religious life of our children harmonize with their social life, so that they may look upon it with spiritual joy and satisfaction, the remembrance of which will linger in their minds long after they have left their alma mater and have become independent members of society.

Instruction in the Bible. Instruction in great religious experiences as taught in the Bible should be given understandingly. Mechanical or rote memorizing of songs, psalms, or chapters, without understanding, had better be avoided. The constant repetition often begets indifference. But fine classical expressions of the virtue of obedience (Samuel's rebuke to Saul); of patriotic devotion (the Jew's lament for Jerusalem when in captivity); of humility (prayers of the Pharisee and the publican); of dependence on God (Solomon's prayer when taking over the kingdom); of personal attachment (Ruth's words to Naomi); of neighborly kindness (story of the Good Samaritan); of God's universal requirement of all men ("He hath showed thee, O man, what is good, and what doth the Lord require of thee but to do justly, love mercy, and walk humbly with thy God"), and many others like them should be taught and memorized understandingly.

Religious Services. The religious services should consist of short morning and evening prayers, grace or recitation of Scripture verses at the meals, and a Sunday afternoon service, the latter often held by a local divine. The services are generally arranged by the committee on devotions of the board, but responsibility for their conduct, as well as all the religious instruction of the girls, lies with the superintendent. In many homes one evening each week is given up to a Christian Endeavor or Girls' Friendly Society which is conducted entirely by the girls. Opportunities should be given for the girls to attend church services at least twice a month and when possible they should be permitted to go to the church of their choice. Catholic girls should be given an opportunity to attend mass and Jewish girls should be permitted to go to the synagogue.

Mental Hygiene. The promotion of mental hygiene in a maternity home is most difficult, yet its importance can not be minimized. On this subject the Children's Bureau of the United States Department of Labor says:

General bodily health is affected by worry and mental strain, and therefore the expectant mother who is building the foundation of her baby's health upon her own should be serene, happy, and cheerful. There is no scientific truth in the belief that a mother can "mark" the baby. Excitement and special causes for anxiety are to be avoided because they disturb the general health. A prospective mother needs to foster her strength, not to waste it.

Workers with unmarried mothers, while realizing the value of this advice, will also realize the difficulty of a girl being "serene, happy, and cheerful" when she is under faced with her serious problems. Some suggestions, however, may be valuable. The girl should be advised:

That the physical welfare of her child may depend largely upon her own mental attitude. She should, therefore, make an effort to forget her own troubles, so that she may be in the best possible condition to bring a normal baby into the world.

That worry never, gets any one anywhere. Brooding over her position and future accomplishes no good results.

That she has not made an irrevocable mistake. While not minimizing the seriousness of her misstep, it should be pointed out that thousands of girls have gone through a similar experience and that many of them are living happy normal lives and occupying places of trust while their children have turned out to be fine men and women.

That they should not talk of their troubles with other girls in the home or listen to the stories of others.

Grammar and High School Instruction. Opportunities should be provided for girls of grammar school and high school age to continue their education while they are in the home. Several methods are used by homes to this end.

(a) By sending the girls to a public school in the neighborhood. In many communities, especially in the West, the girls go from the home direct to the school, where they are not treated any differently than other pupils.

(b) By having the city or county school board supply a teacher who conducts regular classes for the girls in the home, either during the day or in the evenings.

(c) By the superintendent, case worker, or volunteer teacher, who assigns regular home lessons and gives instruction.

Girls capable of profiting by education beyond the high school training which they have completed should be aided. Whether the training desired be collegiate, normal school, vocational, or in some branches of the arts, an effort should be made to enable the girl to have it. Encouragement, wise counsel and, if possible, financial assistance, should be given. It is often possible to interest well-to-do individuals in gifted girls.

Vocational Training. In providing vocational training for girls it should be borne in mind that, although the majority of the girls will probably marry, some will not. Vocational education for women must then train women for both industry and for the home. If it does the former without the latter, it is preparing the average woman for at most only ten years of her future life; if it does the latter alone, it is shirking the needs of those who will continue in industry, and is allowing the temporary workers to stay at ill-paid and unskilled jobs.

Training in the home-making arts is important for a girl not so much because she may need to make her living by doing domestic work, although this is to be considered, but because, in all probability, she will have a home of her own some day; and the success of that home will depend in no small measure upon her ability as a home maker. However, it must be remembered that drudgery is not training, and great care should be taken lest the girl be a victim of the routine of keeping the institution clean. Frequent change of occupation is essential.

Training in cooking should include a study of food values and desirable combinations of food, methods of preparation, and attractive ways of serving. Each girl must have an opportunity to gain experience in actually planning, preparing, and serving meals, under normal conditions and with wise direction.

Special training should be provided for those girls who will have to make their own living. Some of the classes of work which girls will take up, for which they should be trained while in the home, are as follows:

Secretarial Positions. Girls who have completed the high school course and are capable of filling secretarial positions should be assisted to obtain a business education. Many commercial schools offer scholarships or special rates to institutions.

Practical or Registered Nurses. Some girls are trained while in the home as practical nurses. They are enabled to secure work at remunerative wages. Others, after a brief training, enter hospitals or nurses' training schools and secure their diplomas.

Practical Baby Nurses. Girls who are fond of children make excellent baby nurses for whom there is a constant demand. They are especially trained in the nursery for six months to a year.

Recreation Must be Provided. The providing of wholesome recreation for the girls while they are in the home is important. Dr. Miriam Van Waters says: "The program of a correctional institution must turn around a sort of recreational center for self-expression." By teaching the girls how to enjoy themselves by wholesome means while they are in the home, they are not dependent upon cheap commercialized amusement when they leave.

Suggested Recreational Facilities. The following plans for recreation are suggested:

1. Big Sister volunteer groups to act as friendly visitors.

    (a) Such workers to work under the supervision of the social worker of the institution.
    (b) The Big Sisters to provide occasional entertainment in their homes in order to give self-respect and a new outlook to the girls.
    (c) The Big Sisters to be entertained in return by the girls in the institution in order to learn correct social usages.
    (d) Automobile rides in afternoons and evenings to the country.

2. Group singing and music.

    (a) Programs, advice and direction of musical programs are avilable through colleges, schools of music, musical organizations and individual musicians.

3. Out-of-door activities.

    (a) Games such as ball, croquet, etc.
    (b) Hikes and picnics.
    (c) Certain forms of physical culture.
    (d) Gardening.

4. Activities for self-expression.

    (a) Dramatics.
    (b) Arts and crafts.

5. Planned entertainments.

    (a) Regular club meetings conducted by the officers of the Club elected from the girls. Outside speakers are often secured to address these meetings.

    (b) Occasional evening parties planned by the girls with simple prizes to girls who plan the most entertaining evening.

    (c) Birthday party once a month for those whose birthdays come within the month.

6. Cooperation with other organizations.

    (a) Representatives of recreation and program agencies, such as Girl Scouts, Camp Fire Girls, Y. W. C. A., etc., can explain their work to the girls so that upon leaving they will know of the work of the agencies and can affiliate with them.

    (b) Leaders of church societies may visit and become friendly.

Books and Magazines Necessary. Every maternity home should be provided with a library which should contain books of interest to the normal girl as well as books of reference. A request for donations of books once or twice a year will often bring a satisfactory supply, but they should be carefully examined before being placed in the girls' library. Public libraries are often willing to donate duplicates and books that have outlived their usefulness. The facilities of the city public library should be fully used. In addition to supplying desirable books, it often furnishes the following services:

    (a) Periodic visits of a trained librarian.

    (b) Courses of constructive reading lists.

    (c) Advice as to books suitable for individual girls.

    (d) Use of stereopticons and slides both for entertainment and education.

Each girl should be supplied with a Bible of her own. The reading table in the girls' sitting room should be supplied with current magazines.

CHAPTER TWELVE

FOOD AND CLOTHING

Importance of Adequate Diet. The food of the expectant mother and the nursing mother is so important that careful consideration should be given this subject. Many homes for unmarried mothers, largely because of lack of funds, have failed to provide an adequate diet for their inmates. This condition should be remedied. In case resources are not sufficient to permit the right kind and amount of food for all of the inmates their number should be reduced to the number that can be properly fed. In a study of 24 maternity homes in Pennsylvania by the Children's Bureau of the United States Department of Labor it was found that not one home furnished adequate food, either for pregnancy or lastation. Fourteen were classed as "possibly adequate," and the remainder as "probably inadequate" or undetermined. Practically the same situation was found in nine homes in Minnesota.

Careful Study Necessary. Every person responsible for providing the food for expectant and nursing mothers should have some understanding of their requirements and should see that these needs are met as adequately as possible in the dietary. Skilful planning of menus is necessary in order to include the right amount of desirable foods. A study of what the girls actually eat must also be made. Even when adequate food is provided, a girl may have an inadequate diet because she may have the habit of rejecting certain foods. The menus should be selected by the superintendent or matron with the assistance and cooperation of the nurse, and should be submitted to the physician or a dietician at frequent intervals. Assistance in planning a dietary for an institution and advice on the preparation of foods may be secured from offices of the Federal government such as the Children's Bureau, United States Department of Labor, Bureau of Home Economics, and United States Department of Agriculture, all at Washington, D. C.; departments of State economics in State universities, and similar organizations.

Foods that Are Necessary. Milk, eggs, fruit, vegetables and whole-grain cereals are called essential foods and none of them should be omitted.

Milk. The importance of milk as a part of the diet of expectant and nursing mothers is well recognized. The amount should vary from a pint per day for the expectant mothers to a quart for the nursing mothers. Whole milk from tuberculin-tested cows should be used. Cocoa made with milk may be substituted for milk two or three times a week. Some of the milk may be used in custards, puddings, and other cooked foods.

Eggs. Eggs should be served three or four times a week or oftener. An average of seven eggs per week for each girl will generally be sufficient. Eggs may be used to provide a separate dish or in the preparation of other foods, such as custards, salads, etc.

Vegetables. Vegetables should be provided liberally. They must be cooked in a variety of ways and carefully flavored so that the girls may enjoy these important foods. Some vegetable, other than potatoes, should be served at least once every day, preferably twice daily. Leafy vegetables (those from which the leaves and stalks are eaten rather than the fruits,

[166]

roots, or tubers) are especially valuable and should be served three or four times a week. Spinach, kale, and cabbage are cheap and useful. Some uncooked vegetable (as a salad) should be included as often as possible. Potatoes should not be given in place of other vegetables as they are primarily a starchy food; but they may be served daily.

Fruits. Fruits should be served at least once a day. Although dried and canned fruits are an important part of the institution dietary, it is desirable to use some uncooked fruit or vegetable several times a week. Bananas are often cheap and are desirable. Raw apples form a valuable item of diets. Raw tomatoes (as in salads) may take the place of fruits.

Cereals. At least part of the bread served should be whole-wheat, graham, rye, or corn bread. Corn cakes, spoonbread, and waffles make a pleasing diversion. Breakfast cereals should include oatmeal, cream of wheat, etc., which are cooked, as well as dry uncooked cereals, such as corn flakes, rice flakes, shredded wheat, etc.

Meats, Fats and Sugars. A certain amount of each must be given, but none of them should be overused. Meat served four times a week is adequate if fish, eggs, cheese, dried beans or dried peas are substituted for it on other days so that the girls may get the protein which they need. A good weekly plan for the main protein dish of the day would include meat four times, fish once, eggs and cheese once, and dried beans or peas once.

Fats in the diet are valuable and add greatly to its flavor. Butter is a fat which is an especially useful growth food. When every girl is given from a pint to a quart of whole milk daily, she is probably receiving an adequate amount of butterfat; and margarin may be served with the bread if necessary. If part of the milk is skimmed, then an allowance of butter should always be given. Fats should not be used excessively in cooking foods; and fat-rich foods such as pastries are to be avoided.

Starchy and sweet foods are, together with fats, the main sources of energy in the diet. But such foods as bread, potatoes, rice, hominy, macaroni, and other cereals are often given in excess because of their cheapness and substituted for a proportion of the essential foods (meats, fats, green vegetables, and raw fruits). No menu should contain more than two starchy foods as main dishes. Sweet potatoes and yams may take the place of white potatoes, although they are not so nearly equivalent in starch contents as cereals. Sweet dishes in the form of dried or fresh fruits, a prepared milk dessert, or a simple cake such as gingerbread or cookies add to the pleasure of the noon and evening meals, and are at the same time nourishing foods. Some wholesome candy may be given (preferably at a time when it is not likely to diminish the appetite for the next meal).

Adequate and Inadequate Diets. The Children's Bureau of the United States Department of Labor has made the following classification of the daily food plans of homes for unmarried mothers:

Adequate Diet

One pint to 1 quart milk.
One egg.
One serving meat.
One serving leafy vegetable (asparagus, lettuce, greens, cabbage, string beans, etc.).
One serving other vegetable.
One serving potato.
One serving fruit (citrous fruit at least four times a week).
One serving whole-grain cereal.
Four or more slices bread (with butter at three meals).

FOOD AND CLOTHING

Probably Adequate Diet

One cup to 1 pint milk.
One or two servings egg or leafy vegetable.
One serving meat.
One serving other vegetable.
One serving potato.
One serving fruit.
One serving whole-grain cereal.
Bread or other starchy foods with butter.

Possibly Inadequate Diet

One-half cup to 1 cup of milk.
One or two servings egg or leafy vegetable.
One serving meat.
One serving potato or other vegetable.
One serving fruit.
Bread or other starchy foods, with some butter.

Probably Inadequate Diet

Milk in coffee to one-half cup.
One or two servings egg or meat.
One or two servings vegetable or fruit.
One serving potato.
Bread or other starchy foods, with small amount butter or butter substitute.

Planning the Menus. The menus should be planned at least a week in advance, preferably several weeks; and certain general principles must be kept in mind.

(a) Menus should be arranged with the idea of including in each day's food plan adequate amounts of the right foods. It is essential to use the week as the unit in making out menus because certain foods (such as eggs) are not always used daily.

(b) Variety is so important an element in making food attractive that great care should be taken not to serve the same dishes on the same days of the week. A file should be kept of all the daily menus served. Repetition can be avoided by a careful study of this file. It should be augmented constantly as new methods of preparing foods are adopted and changes made in flavorings, and as the food materials vary from season to season.

(c) The food must be properly distributed among the meals of the day. Supper or lunch must not be too light and dinner too heavy, nor the reverse. It is not desirable to concentrate in one meal the greater part of the required food. For nursing mothers lunches consisting of milk and crackers may be provided twice daily in addition to the regular meals.

Suggested Menus for One Week. The following menus for a week are given to illustrate the generous use of vegetables, especially leafy vegetables, and the use of milk, eggs, and cheese in cooking:

Monday:
  Breakfast—Sliced bananas, toast, sliced bacon, coffee.
  Dinner—Macaroni and cheese, corn on cob, escalloped potatoes, cabbage salad, gingerbread with whipped cream.
  Supper—Stuffed baked potatoes (meat and potatoes), "butterfly" salad with mayonnaise dressing, frosted cookies, applesauce, coffee or tea.
Tuesday:
  Breakfast—Raw apple, cereal, toast, coffee.
  Dinner—Hamburger steak, buttered carrots, mashed potatoes, beet pickles, tapioca.
  Supper—Egg and lettuce salad, bran muffins, pear sauce, coconut cake, coffee, or tea.
Wednesday:
  Breakfast—French toast, cereal, apple butter, coffee.
  Dinner—Roast veal with dressing, riced potatoes, stewed tomatoes, peach salad with date in center (black-eyed Susan), apple pie with cheese.
  Supper—Welsh rarebit on toast, combination salad (lettuce, cucumbers, tomatoes), gelatin, drop cookies, coffee or tea.
Thursday:
  Breakfast—Scrambled eggs, stewed apricots, toast, coffee.
  Dinner—Meat pie, sweet potatoes, head-lettuce salad with Thousand Island dressing, creamed string beans, prune whip with custard sauce.
  Supper—Sardine-salad sandwiches, radish and lettuce salad, apple snow, vanilla wafers, coffee.
Friday:
  Breakfast—Pancakes, stewed prunes, toast, coffee.

Dinner—Baked trout, escalloped potatoes, spinach, tomato and bean salad, chocolate pudding.

Supper—Creamed salmon on toast, cheese salad, Bavarian cream, chocolate cake, coffee or tea.

Saturday:

Breakfast—Milk toast, jam, toast, coffee.

Dinner—Baked beans, browned potatoes, buttered peas, apricot and coconut salad, caramel custard.

Supper—Spanish rice, cottage-cheese salad, muffins, sherbet with vanilla wafers, coffee or tea.

Sunday:

Breakfast—One-half orange, cereal, toast, coffee.

Dinner—Pot roast, riced potatoes, carrots and peas creamed, pineapple and tomato salad, baked apple with whipped cream.

Supper—Cold sliced meat, potato salad, pickles or relish, cake, cherry sauce, coffee or tea.

Diet During Lactation. The diet during lactation should be increased. Lunches consisting of milk, crackers, and cheese should be provided at 10 A. M., 3 P. M., and at bedtime for the nursing mothers.

Same Kind of Food for Workers and Inmates. The same kind of food should be provided for workers and girls, and there should be no provision for special dishes, unless by orders of the physicians, and then they should not be served at the regular meals. Dr. Barrett had firm convictions on this subject. She said:

Sometimes we are told that the food which would be all right for the girls is not of a kind that will suit the superintendent or other workers. Then I should say, change your food. Any woman who is physically able to fulfill the arduous duties of an officer in a maternity home would necessarily have a digestion sufficiently strong to assimilate good wholesome food. If for any particular reason a diet has been prescribed for her, of course an exception should be made, and she should be permitted to have her meals either in her room or at a different hour from the other members of the family. It is needless to explain to intelligent people how harmful discrimination of foods may be in a home where they have maternity cases. We profess to take these girls in our home, and treat them as we would like others to treat our own daughters, if they were in similar circumstances. This means a great deal, and we have to be very careful that the girls can not pick flaws in our professions. In this respect we point to the Great Example. We never could have imagined Christ eating at a different table from His disciples, nor could we have imagined Him feeding the multitude on bread and fishes while He manufactured dainties for Himself.

Cost of Food. The cost of raw food will depend largely upon the location of the institution and the seasons of the year. In some small communities, the price of milk and vegetables which form an important part of the diet is much lower than in large cities. Some institutions have supporters among butchers, wholesale green grocers, bakers, fish dealers and dairies, who supply food at cost or even below cost at times. The planting of gardens and the keeping of chickens or cows often reduce the outlay of cash. Donations of food at Thanksgiving and Christmas materially reduce the financial outlay. Taking the country as a whole, and buying all the raw food, including milk, at current wholesale prices, the average cost per adult per day should be between 32 and 45 cents.[1]

Clothing. The standard for dress for a girl in a maternity home should be as high as that for the average girl in the community in which the home is located.

Uniforms Undesirable. Uniforms or special costumes set the girl apart and should not be used. On the subject of clothing in general, Dr. Barrett wrote:

While our girls do not wear uniforms or anything else as a mark of their position, and are permitted to wear their own clothes, if they have suitable

[1] "Standards for Maternity Hospitals," issued by the Children's Bureau of the State Board of Control, St. Paul, Minn., contains valuable suggestions on the subject of food values. A copy may be obtained on request.

articles, yet we insist that during the week they should all wear washable dresses. There is nothing more depressing than a number of women, many of whose faces bear the marks of disease, dressed in woolen clothes that can not be readily cleansed. The atmosphere seems full of germs, as it frequently is, for we shrink more or less from contagion when we fall in with a company gathered from the byways and hedges. On the other hand, to see a girl dressed in a ten-cent gingham, neatly made, rustling in its spick-and-span-ness, is exhilarating, like a breath of fresh air.

While we require this style of dress from the girls, we do not forget that we must teach them, by example as well as precept, in the manner of dress, as well as in other things. We must not forget that a fondness for dress has often been the cause of a woman's downfall, and in no way is her looseness of morals shown in a more pronounced manner than in her style of dress after her downfall. For this reason, every one who comes in contact with our girls in an official manner needs to encourage simplicity of dress, with extreme neatness. Not long since I went to see an industrial exhibition at a State institution. The teacher of one of the industrial classes of girls was dressed in a delicate silk dress trimmed with lace and made in elaborate style. On her fingers gleamed innumerable rings, and her hair was done up in a most elaborate coiffure. She was teaching a class of girls from 14 to 18 years of age who were dressed in an ugly prison-like garb. No doubt, to their eyes, she appeared a vision of beauty, and three-fourths of them were saying in their hearts, "When I get out of here, I shall have dresses and rings like hers." They had been taught to look upon her as their model and why should they not think that her style of dress was quite the proper thing for wage-earning women to wear? The teacher was a pretty woman, but I could not help thinking that if she had been dressed in a simple wash gown, how different the effect upon those girls' minds would have been. They would have said in just the same way, "When I am out of here, I am going to have a dress just like that to wear," and sure enough when they went to work they could well have afforded one and have earned the money honestly to pay for it. On the other hand, to have the elaborate costume, in a majority of cases, they would have to earn the money dishonestly, and at best would have been spending a larger proportion of their earnings for clothes than good sense would dictate.

We have adopted in our home for our matron a costume that is pretty and cheap. It is all white. A white duck or piqué skirt with white shirt-waists for special occasions. The assistant matron and the workers in the home all wear solid blue gingham with white aprons with straps across the shoulders, and a dainty little cap.

[173]

We also provide striped gingham dresses, white aprons, and caps for those who are heads of departments.

The cap and apron in our home are a badge of authority. Therefore when our girls go out in positions, they naturally fall into the use of the cap and apron, when they are asked to wear them, and do not feel that in any sense it is a badge of inferiority. Soldiers, sailors, and policemen are all proud of their uniforms; why should not the pretty, becoming, and serviceable cap and apron be looked upon with pride instead of being considered a mark of servitude?

In some homes where there are organized troops of Girl Scouts, Camp Fire Girls, etc., the members wear the uniforms of these organizations. In other homes, the girls wear "smocks" of various colors during the day.

Street Clothing Necessary. For attendance at church, shopping, visits to the doctors, etc., street clothing is necessary in addition to working and house clothes. Wraps, gloves, and overshoes should be adequate for the climate. No girl should be compelled to wear garments that are out of date, outgrown, or in bad repair. Articles that are out of date should be remodeled or discarded. Those which are in bad repair should be discarded if they can not be satisfactorily mended. Routine mending should regularly follow laundering. Garments should be marked. A record of the clothing given to each girl is desirable. Having garments plainly marked makes it easy to return to each girl the same clothes after laundering and mending. The sense of ownership which this gives is an important element in the development and maintenance of self-respect and personal pride. Personal responsibility for clothes will also be more readily accepted. Girls should be taught to mend their clothes. Responsibility for at least the simpler processes of repair will help to emphasize taking care of clothes and being responsible for their condition.

Baby Layettes.[1]   Every girl should be taught to make the layette for her own baby. The following list gives the clothing necessary for the average new-born baby:

Diapers, dozen	4 to 8
Knitted bands, number	2 to 4
Knitted shirts, number	2 to 4
Flannel petticoats, number	2 to 4
Nightgowns, number	3
White cotton slips, number	4 to 8
Coat and caps	
Long bootees or stockings, pairs	2 to 4
Sacques, number	3
Wraps or blankets, number	3

Methods of Securing Clothing.   Maternity homes must largely depend upon donations of clothing to supply the needs of the girls.   In many homes there is a sewing circle of ladies which meets at the home monthly or oftener and spends the entire day in sewing for the girls and helping them make and remodel their clothing, as well as instructing them in fancy work, embroidery, etc.   Many of the fancy articles so made are sold to provide funds for materials.   The Needlework Guild in many communities furnish bed clothing, table linen, towels, baby layettes, etc.   Church societies are often glad to send needed articles.   A source of valuable clothing, coats and sweaters, especially hats and shoes, are girls' boarding schools and colleges.   Many girl students, when going home for the holidays or at the end of the school term, have excellent articles of clothing which they are ready to discard, and a request that they be sent to the home generally brings excellent results.

Outfit on Leaving the Home.   An effort should be made to provide every girl who leaves the home with a complete outfit of clothing for herself and baby, in case she or her friends are unable to supply it.

---

[1] "Infant Care," published by the U. S. Children's Bureau, Washington, which can be obtained free on request, contains valuable suggestions as to the proper clothing for babies.

CHAPTER THIRTEEN

SCHEDULE OF ACTIVITIES

Definite Schedule Advisable. A definite schedule of activities is desirable in order to distribute the work among the girls, allow them to nurse and care for their babies, give adequate time for rest and recreation, and provide for hours for school, religious and other instruction. The schedule should be fixed by the superintendent after consultation with the matron and nurse, and should be submitted to the physician. It should be revised from time to time according to the climate, seasons of the year, number and capabilities of the girls, and other conditions which are fluctuating.

Assignment of Duties. Every girl should be assigned specific duties. This assignment should be made by the superintendent after consultation with the matron and nurse. A daily conference of these officers when these assignments are discussed is advisable. Changes in assignments should be frequent. No girl should be kept in the same position for more than a month, except under special circumstances. Exceptions should be made, of course, to girls who are taking special training in nursing, as they should be in the hospital or nursery as long as possible, but this special training should not commence until they have completed their various assignments in all of the other departments of the home.

Division of Work. The principal divisions of work to which the various girls may be assigned are as follows:

(a) Cleaners and scrubbers.
(b) Laundry workers.
(c) Cooks.
(d) Pantry maid.
(e) Dish washers and wipers.
(f) Hospital attendant.
(g) Nurses in nursery.
(h) Office assistant.
(i) Librarian.
(j) Parlor and reception maid.

Suggested Routine. The following routine of a well-conducted maternity home is suggested for study:

6:00 A. M.   Rising hour.
6:30 A. M.   Breast feeding. (All babies are nursed 20 minutes unless mother is otherwise ordered by physician in charge. Babies are weighed before and after nursing. All mothers are required to express remaining milk after each nursing, and the breast milk thus obtained is used to complement the food of the babies needing it.)
7:30 A. M.   Breakfast. (All patients must be fully dressed.)
8:00 A. M.   Bathe and weigh babies. (Under supervision of nurse, each baby is examined daily for rash, sore throat or any unusual symptoms.)
8:30 A. M.   Report for duties.
10:30 A. M.   Breast feeding (same as 6:30 A. M.).
10:50 A. M.   Babies are placed in baskets and put out-of-doors if weather permits.
11:00 A. M.   Study hour.
12:00 M.   Dinner.
12:45 P. M.   Report for duties.
2:30 P. M.   Breast feeding (same as 6:30 A. M.).
2:50 P. M.   Free for rest or recreation.
3:45 P. M.   Study period.
5:15 P. M.   Undress babies for night. Before putting on baby's night clothes let him kick and play a few minutes on bed.
5:30 P. M.   Supper.

6:30 P. M.   Breast feeding (same as 6:30 A. M.).
7:00 P. M.   Prayers.
10:30 P. M.   Breast feeding (same as 6:30 A. M.).
10:50 P. M.   Lights out.
2:30 A. M.   Breast feeding (this feeding should not be given after first two months).

Girls assigned as cooks and pantry maid should go on duty at 6:45 A. M., 10:45 A. M., and 4 P. M. When a three-hour feeding schedule is required, it will be necessary to change the hours suggested above.

One Day In Detail. The following outline of a day in a maternity home by Dr. Barrett is interesting:

I am sure by giving you the features of one day in detail, you will have a clearer idea of the ease with which our work goes on.

Every good housekeeper knows that in order to have a successful day, it must begin the night before. The oatmeal is washed and put to soak, and if there be hash or potato cakes it is all prepared ready to be cooked. This, with bread, butter and coffee is our usual morning meal. As our family is very large, everybody rises at six o'clock. The girls get up, dress themselves, and if they have babies, bathe and dress them also before breakfast, except the dining room and kitchen girls, whose babies are taken directly to the nursery and cared for by the nursery maids, as their duties prevent them from attending to them early in the morning. Each girl folds her bed clothes and hangs them on the chair to air. She does not make her bed; that is done by those in charge of the bed-room work.

We have a short prayer and the Doxology before we sit down to breakfast. While breakfast is being eaten, the matron gives to the girls any instructions that she desires in regard to the division of labor for the day. The girls in the different departments are exchanged once a month, with the exception of the heads of the kitchen and the laundry, who generally occupy those positions a longer time. After breakfast, the girls go cheerfully to the work that has been given to them. At ten o'clock the hardest part of the work for the day is over, and everybody is beginning to feel just a little weary. It is a glad, happy break in the day when the bell rings for all to repair to the sitting room for the hour of Bible study and school work. This feature of the day is the great harmonizing factor in the home. While bodies are resting, souls are being fed by the word of God, and in the singing of the sweet hymns and in the ascending

[179]

prayers much of the friction of the day has been lost. Everybody returns to work with renewed vigor, and thus we often say that we get twenty-five hours out of the twenty-four.

We must pause here to admit an inmate. A girl mounts the front steps and timidly rings the bell. She feels as if the eyes of every passerby on the street are riveted upon her, and that each one knows her secret. She does not realize that every day a dozen or more ladies and young girls, workers in the Master's vineyard, mount these same steps, and that there is nothing different in her appearance to mark her from them. The door opens and she is greeted by a trim girl whose badge of authority is a neat white apron and muslin cap. She is not stared at as an object of curiosity, as she half feared, but is cordially asked to enter, and is treated as an expected and welcome guest. She is shown into the drawing room, and as she sits down there greets her every evidence of the fact that this is a true home—God's home—and she feels insensibly the safety and the comfort of being cared for, which the very atmosphere of love seems to breathe forth. The superintendent comes in to greet her. She is cordial, at the same time not oppressively so, but there is that willingness to help and that self-reliant courage in her bearing that at once makes the girl feel that she is to be depended upon. The superintendent does not begin by asking her a long string of questions, but simply says, "Can I be of any help to you?" Touched by the tenderness of her tone, in a few moments the girl has sobbed out her sin and her needs. She is assured that it does not matter what the past has been, the future may be all that she desires to make it, if only she is faithful in her resolves and is willing to be guided by the friends that she now has found. For her encouragement she is reminded of how wonderfully God can use her experience in helping and warning others, when she herself has gotten firmly established in her new life. She is told that this is a home for the girls; that it belongs to the girls; that it belongs to her; that it does not belong to the board, or the president or the superintendent, but to the girls; and that all required of any is that each one shall do her part in making it a real home. She is told that while one person can not make a home, one person may do much towards marring a home. She is told that she must not discuss the sorrows and sins of her past, but that if at any time she needs advice or comfort, she is free to come to the superintendent and receive it. She is made to understand that she is not pauperized by coming into the home, and that she must not feel that she is accepting alms; that she will have an opportunity when she has been established in right paths to repay to the home all that it has done for her, and not only that, but that she will be able to do for others who may need a home. She is made to feel that what will be done for her is not for any earthly reward, but for Christ's sake, and that the only way she can repay it is, not only by money, but by showing a willing spirit; that all the recompense which we desire is to see her saved and taking her place on the side of right. Nothing is more debilitating to a highstrung girl than to feel that she is an object to charity, and after all it is these highstrung girls who are going to be our star cases, if we can only get them into right paths. I have often felt, when I have noticed the restlessness of girls to get out of a home, that it often comes from the fact that those in authority do not make them feel that the home is theirs, and that they are honestly earning their own living when they do what they are asked, whether that be much or little, or whether it brings in a penny or not.

Dinner is at half-past twelve. For dinner we always have a good meat, two or three kinds of vegetables, and dessert three times a week. Immediately after dinner, the superintendent calls all the workers and the heads of the departments for a daily conference. At this conference all the difficulties that are met with by each one in their various departments are brought forward and discussed, and methods are adopted to make the work more harmonious and successful. The characteristics of the different girls are discussed in their various positions, and their limitations are kindly but firmly commented upon. It is impossible to have unity of effort without these conferences. "Two heads are better than one," and it is no matter how clever and consecrated a superintendent may be, she needs the advice and help of her coworkers. If she is not willing to receive it and to be modified by their influence she is a dangerous person to have at the head of any organization, because it will surely be run into a rut and become a one woman's work—a most unfortunate dilemma to contemplate. The ideal superintendent needs to have an open mind and an open heart. "An open mind to recognize facts, and an open heart to give sympathetic interpretation to these facts." You will say that we want something in our superintendent that is beyond human. Yes, it is far beyond human that we desire; but there is One who "giveth freely and upbraideth not," who is ready to enlarge our human limitations.

The afternoon is usually devoted to work in the school room and the sewing room. We have educational classes or Bible study classes about two hours each day.

Supper is at 5 o'clock, and we usually serve bread and butter, tea, and some sort of relish, the meal being followed by a religious service, the girls each repeating one or more verses of Scripture, followed by singing and prayer.

Immediately after supper the girls go to the nursery and take their babies and put them to bed. The girls are permitted to retire as soon as they please after things are put in order for the night, except on the evenings when services are held.

Mr. Moody always insisted that, at the Bible Institute, there should be one "Play Night" in the week, in which all Bible study was laid aside, the students engaging in simple games and amusements for recreation. If such a break in the routine of the week was necessary for the class of students that Mr. Moody gathered about him, how necessary it is that we should not forget the social side of life in our homes, where the majority of our family are young people. One night in the week should be set aside for this purpose. Some little treat, such as apples, peanuts or candy should be provided, and a social time enjoyed. We find many kind friends to help us out in this line. One week the Y. W. C. A. come and always bring some pretty little souvenirs and some one to sing or play. The Daughters of the King help on other weeks. In addition to these societies, there are a number of individuals who, knowing that Monday night is our play night, come in to spend a social hour with us. Sunday is a real rest day in the home for the girls. Everything that is possible has been done the day before, and the rules are very lax for Sunday. Our girls who are out at work come to visit us, and the girls have the privilege that day of taking the babies from the nursery to their own rooms. The counterpanes are taken from the beds and the girls are permitted to lie down in the afternoon. At 3 o'clock we have our evangelistic service which everybody is expected to attend. These services are conducted by clergymen from different denominations, who bring with them their choir, and frequently other assistants. Our girls are not taken out to church until after they have been with us for six months, then if we feel that they have made a beginning in a new life, they are encouraged to connect themselves with some denomination; our workers, representing the different evangelistic bodies, accompany them to the church of their choice. We think that a great deal is accomplished by completely isolating them from the outside world during the first few months of their sojourn with us. It is a great help in having them break all outside ties completely, and to teach them to have resources within themselves. They soon become interested in the simple home pleasures that we give them, and entirely weaned from the reckless life of excitement in which they have lived in the past. This must first be accomplished as a good foundation for future character building.

We have what we call our Honor Class, and to belong to this class is a great incentive to conscientious effort on the part of the girls. Every member of this class must have made conscientious effort to do right for at least six months to be considered eligible to it. She must have shown herself to be truthful, reliable, and trustworthy. When she is admitted to the class, her privileges are increased. She is permitted to go out alone occasionally, has her afternoon to herself as the workers have, and is looked upon as worthy of emulation. No spirit of rivalry is excited by this, because every girl is eligible to the class if she will only behave herself in such a way as to deserve it. Everything that stimulates honest effort, or which leads to greater usefulness, should be encouraged in the home. Most of all, our girls want to be made to feel that they are making progress in regaining their lost position in the eyes of the world, as well as in the eyes of God.

There are no drones in our home. Every girl is expected to do her share in each department of the work unless she is physically disabled from doing so. If she is unable to do laundry work, we usually ask some one to volunteer to take her place, and it is beautiful to see how willing the girls are to do for one another when one can not do for herself. This is shown in their generosity in dividing their belongings, and any little money that they may have, with one another.

There are no favorites in our home. If a girl comes in who is educated and refined in appearance, and who has had better advantages than the majority who come to us, instead of being petted and given an easy position because of this, she is really less excusable for being in such a home as ours than the dirty, unkempt child of the tenements, who has never known anything but degradation. Possibly the first real home that such as she has ever known will be our home, and it is a rare privilege indeed to be permitted to open up to such a one as this avenues of a truly womanly life.

If a girl comes to us well dressed and with manicured nails and tells us that she has never been accustomed to do any sort of work in her life, we are sure to put this girl at the wash tub, because we will never be able to do anything with her until she has learned to believe in the aristocracy of hard hands, and the dignity of labor.

Our family being large, it requires three girls in the kitchen in the busy part of the day to do the work properly. The head of the kitchen is, of course, the cook, who attends to the fire and does all the cooking; the second girl helps the cook to prepare the vegetables and get the food ready for the oven; the third girl keeps the kitchen clean and washes all the utensils as soon as they are soiled, and all three assist in serving the meal. The tables and sink are covered with zinc, which shines as if it were silver. The floor is scrubbed every day, and the windows washed three times a week. Every piece of tin and every piece of woodwork is dusted every day as carefully as if it were bric-a-brac in a drawing room. The work is so systematized that there is not the least confusion when it comes the time for serving the meals. Everybody knows her part, and the kitchen is as neat while a meal is being served as it is when it is placed in order for the night. This we look upon as a most important feature, because there is nothing more discouraging to one when she has eaten a hearty meal, and feels like sitting down to digest it, than to be compelled to clean up a whole lot of soiled dishes that have been permitted to accumulate during the busy hours of the day.

The laundry is a very important feature in every home, and usually in institutions similar to ours, it is frequently one of the unsolved problems; but owing to the democratic spirit of our home, we have no trouble whatever with the laundry, because everybody does her share of it. We believe that every lady should know how to cook, wash, and iron, if she does not know anything else, and as we expect our girls to be ladies in the highest and truest sense, they must all learn to do these things and do them well. Each girl is required to wash her own clothes and her baby's, if she has one; also her bed linen and towels. In addition to this, so many girls are detailed each week to do the washing from the ward, the table linen and the officers' wash, as well as the general wash from the nursery, except the soiled clothes, which are washed each day. In this way the burden is not heavy upon any one, and the stigma which generally attaches to being "sent to the laundry" as a sort of punishment, is removed. Even our workers who come to us for training are expected to do their own laundry, as we have learned that it is impossible for one to teach another what she herself does not know by experience.

There is one girl in charge of the laundry, and it is her duty to make all the starch, to distribute the soap, and to see that no one is wasteful with the hot water. She has charge of the laundry fire and the distribution of irons, and sees that everything is in its proper place and the laundry neat when the work is finished. If any friction arises between the girls, she reports it to the matron. She is responsible for all the clothes sent to the laundry, and sees that they are neatly laundered and returned in good condition to the linen closet.

The laundry may also be made a remunerative feature of the home by taking in outside work. One of our homes is a notable example of what may be accomplished by a well-conducted laundry. Each month they clear enough money in the laundry to pay all the running expenses of the home, outside of rents. The girls appreciate the opportunity of earning money for the home, and in order that they may see the fruits of their labor, we would recommend that the money which they receive for it should be expended in such a way that they may have tangible evidences of what their labor has accomplished. If any luxuries are indulged in, let them come from the girls' labors.

Apart from its remunerative features, the laundry may also be used as "a means of grace." There is nothing that settles a restless, highstrung spirit like weariness of the flesh. To many of our girls, accustomed to an active life and full of the fire of youth, manual labor is a necessity, and while no branch of work should be permitted to sink into drudgery, nor any one be allowed to overwork, at the same time everybody should be so tired when they go to bed that sleep should naturally follow and bring the required rest. Much of the restlessness and many of the mischievous pranks which bring our homes into ill repute would be prevented if we were wiser in utilizing the animal spirits of our charges in some wise and profitable manner.

CHAPTER FOURTEEN

LEGAL ASSISTANCE

Responsibility of Maternity Agencies. Agencies dealing with the unmarried mother have a definite responsibility to see that the proper legal machinery is set in motion for the protection of the girl and baby under their charge, as well as to the public in general. This responsibility may be summed up as follows:

1. To see that every birth is registered and a birth certificate issued. This certificate should not show that the child is illegitimate, and most States now issue a certificate which simply states the name of the mother, and does not mention her marital relations.

2. To institute proceedings that will establish the paternity of the child and its legitimation by acknowledgment of the father, or by marriage if the latter is deemed for the best interests of the girl and the child.

3. To secure from the putative father financial and other assistance to cover the mother's expenses for confinement and for the support of the child.

4. To secure assistance from public funds, as that provided for the indigent poor, mothers' pensions, etc., when the girl and her child are in need of such assistance.

5. To institute criminal proceedings in all cases of seduction, rape, incest, etc.

Study of the Laws Desirable. A study of the laws on illegitimacy and allied subjects should be made by those in charge of agencies for the assistance of the unmarried mother so that they may be familiar with all of the remedies that are provided. A summary of the laws and their principal provisions is given in Chapter Five. A copy of the State laws may generally be secured by application to the Children's Bureau of each State.

Necessity of Securing Cooperation of Girl and Her Friends. One of the greatest difficulties in the way of securing such legal remedy as is provided by the laws for the unmarried mother and her child is the reluctance of the girl to appear in court, and the desire on the part of many social workers "to shield the girl." This is a matter that requires careful consideration and delicate handling. It should not be discussed until the girl has been in the home for a sufficient time to feel that those in charge are her friends, and that any action proposed is for her best interest. It should be pointed out that for the child's sake action should be taken to have its paternity established, and to secure from its father such support as will enable it to receive the care that should be expected from a legal parent. In cases of seduction, rape, and incest, the responsibility of the girl to join in such proceedings as will deter similar attempts on other girls should be dwelt upon.

Methods of Procedure. The responsibility for securing legal relief should rest with an officer or member of the board, or with the social worker. In many instances, boards have among their members a lawyer who takes charge of this work. In others the services of a volunteer lawyer are secured. The first step to be taken is to establish friendly relations with the civil authorities in order that the fullest cooperaion may be secured.

CHAPTER FIFTEEN

RECORDS AND STATISTICS

The Purpose of Records and Statistics. Every institution caring for the unmarried mother and her child should have a record system by which may be known definitely the problems with which it deals, the details of its management and its accomplishments. It should have its data in such shape that requests for information from city, county, and State authorities, social agencies, and its own members can be easily and accurately furnished.

Simple System Desirable. To accomplish the ends suggested above a simple system is desirable. Many institutions have cumbersome systems which are unnecessary and require the services of clerical assistance beyond their resources.

Elements of a Simple System. For effective records the following system is suggested for the average maternity home:

1. Admission record. This should be printed on a card, 5 by 8 inches, and should contain the entry of facts which are frequently needed. The entries on this card are of two kinds:

   (a) Permanent facts which serve to identify the family, such as names, date and place of birth, nationality, and previous addresses.
   (b) Facts which may change with further developments and which give an outline of the social situation, such as wages, physical and mental condition, occupation, and school grade.

A sample of this form is shown in Exhibit 1 in the appendix.

2. Current record. This consists of a form, generally of four pages each, 8 by 11 inches, upon which are entered reports

of investigations and interviews. It contains informaton as to the girl's residence, family, school record, occupation before entering home, information regarding the father of her child, court history, sex experiences, circumstances surrounding her trouble, history while she is in the home, and space for record of the disposition of the girl and her baby and subsequent history. A sample of a record of this kind is shown in Exhibit 2 in the appendix.

3. Physical record. The physical record should have complete data regarding the physical condition of the girl and the baby while she is in the home. Form 3 (shown in the appendix), which covers the record of labor and delivery, includes the previous physical history which might influence the present pregnancy and a record of the present physical examination. Form 4 is a record of the nursing care and postpartum examination of the mother and baby. In the event the patient is sent from the maternity home to the hospital, a record such as suggesed in Form 5 should be used, and this should be sent to the hospital and returned by the hospital when the girl and her baby are returned to the home.

4. Visitors' Record. A record should be kept of all visitors.

5. Diary showing number of inmates; meals served to workers and inmates; contributions of food and clothing received, and similar data.

6. Financial Records. A complete record of all receipts and disbursements, and list of subscribers should be kept.

Methods of Keeping Records. The admission records should be kept in a card index file and the cards should be filed alphabetically. A vertical letter file should be provided for the keeping of the current and physical record and a separate folder should be used for each inmate. In this folder, in addition to the two records, should be kept all correspondence with friends and relatives of the girl, as well as letters received from her after she leaves the institution. These folders may be filed alphabetically or by number. Bound books should be used for all financial transactions. All records should be kept under lock and key.

Who Should Keep Records. The admission and current record and diary should be kept by the superintendent. Entries on the current record should be made by the social worker or person who is charged with the responsibility of making investigations and doing the follow-up work. The physical record should be kept by the nurse. The treasurer should keep the financial records as well as the list of the contributors to the institution. The superintendent should keep a cash book showing the amount of money received by her for admission fees and expenditures for food, supplies, etc., authorized by the board. A numbered receipt book should be used by the superintendent for acknowledging all admission fees, and the stub of this receipt book should show the amount and dates of payment and from whom received.

Audit of Books Necessary. A complete audit of the books of the superintendent and treasurer should be made at least annually by a competent auditor who is not officially connected with the institution. The records of the superintendent should be examined at intervals by some member of the board in order to see that they are properly kept.

Annual Report Should Be Made. An annual report should be made to the board covering all of the transactions that have taken place during the year, and a copy of this report should be sent to city, county, and State authorities, national organizations with which the home is affiliated, subscribers, etc.

Inviolability of Records. While it is extremely desirable to cooperate with other social agencies, and to give and receive from them all information through social service exchange or other organizations that may help in solving the problems of the girl and her child, great care should be exercised in furnishing information contained in the records. Each request for information should be specific, and only such information given out as will answer that inquiry. No member of the board, social worker, public official, or any other person should be permitted to go through the records indiscriminately in search of information. The superintendent should be extremely careful in discussing the individual histories of girls, even with members of the board, unless she has a particular object in view that will help to solve a problem.

CHAPTER SIXTEEN

MISCELLANEOUS MATTERS OF POLICY

Attitude Towards Mother's Assuming Status of Legitimate Mother. Perhaps no policy of agencies dealing with the unmarried mother is more difficult to define than that of advising girls as to the attitude they should take in assuming the status of a legitimate mother. The social worker is confronted by two considerations, first, the necessity of protecting the girl and her child born out of wedlock, and second, the safeguarding of the interests of the legal family. The second of these has been stated by Dr. Ada E. Sheffield as follows:

> The stigma which rests upon the mother and the child is inseparable from society's respect for monogamy. As for this stigma, just so long as it adds to our self-respect to think of our own parents as having observed custom and the moral law, just so long will it be impossible for us to feel an equal respect for those persons whose misfortune it is to have parents who did not observe the moral law.

Taking another point of view, Prof. Ernst Freund has said:

> The view that the interest of the child is the paramount interest to which all other considerations should yield is not only attractive but socially sound. The view, on the other hand, that in the interest of the institution of marriage the fruit of illicit relations must be penalized and made odious is intrinsically abhorrent.

The general attitude of practically all social workers who have considered the subject is that no great progress can be made in the moral regeneration of an unmarried mother who lives a life of deception. Furthermore they agree that the constant fear of discovery of the secret of her experience has an effect upon a girl that colors her whole life. Therefore they counsel a frank and honest disclosure of the facts when necessary. They insist upon a full disclosure of all the facts to immediate relatives, prospective husbands, and (in most instances) employers.

The Children's Bureau of the United States Department of Labor in investigating this subject says:

The ethical problems presented in case work with unmarried mothers are very grave, and they are fraught with perplexing difficulties on every hand. Social workers often honestly desire to refrain from cooperation in these deceptions, yet they feel powerless to direct the mothers in a wiser course. To say that in order to be successful and to establish enduring relationships on a basis of truth is one thing, but to go so far as to assume responsibility for engineering the lives of human beings towards this end is a different matter. The conscientious social worker who seriously contemplates the position of the mother and child will usually hesitate to go further than to advise—perhaps insist upon—honesty in intimate relationship, such as with close relatives, families who employ the mothers in their homes, and prospective husbands.

The attitude of many social workers is expressed in the following statement by the head of a maternity home:

First: We put pressure upon the girl to acknowledge her condition to those people immediately concerned with her, i. e., parents, or, if she is planning to marry, the man himself.

Second: We do not put pressure on her to call herself wife or widow, but we do cooperate with the concealment by addressing her as "Mrs." when writing, or in other ways where we feel that a knowledge of her true status would expose her to aggression on the part of the community.

I realize fully that this compromise may retard the education of the public at large, and so share in the old-fashioned policy of concealment, but at the same time I feel that the girl is by public opinion placed at such disadvantage in her upward struggle that she deserves some privileged treatment for her protection.

While consenting to this, however, we really do try to get over to the girls the essentials of the square deal, both with the relatives and the prospective husbands, and the paramount importance of facing close relationships on an honest basis.

Dr. Barrett gave considerable thought to this subject. She said:

The question is often asked us, "How much do you tell of a girl's history to her employer?" How much we tell them depends entirely upon the girl. If it is the first time she has been out in a position, and if there are certain weaknesses in her character that need to be strengthened, we would always put such a case with a woman who is sufficiently wise to be trusted with the history of the girl. But we feel that whatever is told should be told by the superintendent or case worker to the lady herself; that under no circumstances should the girl be permitted to tell her own story to any one, and that the mistress should never discuss the subject with her, or allude to the fact that she has been an unfortunate girl.

While we believe in doing everything possible to protect our girls from the curiosity of unwise questioners, we make them understand very clearly that they are always to speak the truth and not to permit the fear of some one discovering the truth about them lead them into telling falsehoods or misleading persons. Everybody has a right to discuss, or not, their private affairs, and the world is entitled to know that only which it can find out by watching the actions of persons. The Constitution of the United States asserts that everybody has an equal right to the pursuit of life, liberty, and happiness. We try to impress upon our girls the fact that they must not discuss their fall with any one; that if some one should ask them anything in regard to their past life they should say with quiet dignity, "I have had a great deal of trouble in my life and it only brings up painful memories to discuss the subject." No one whose good opinion is worth having would care to peer beneath such reticence.

The question as to whether an unmarried mother should be advised to adopt the title of "Mrs." and to wear a wedding ring are ones that give social workers much concern. Personally, the writer believes that girls should be told that there is no objection to the use of either of these subterfuges. There

[195]

are no legal restrictions to such actions. Men are not compelled to disclose their marital relationship either by using a distinctive title in front of their names or by wearng a wedding ring and women should not have any greater handicap.

Censoring Mail. One of the policies that must be settled by maternity homes is that of censoring mail. There is a difference of opinion among social workers as to this practice. In a recent conference of superintendents of maternity homes, it was found that one-half censored the mail of the girls and the rest did not. It was claimed by those who favored the practice that they could not control the girls and plan for their future if they were permitted to receive letters from persons who were suggesting plans at variance with the policy of the institution. On the other hand, opponents of the practice claimed that censoring mail destroyed the spirit of confidence between the girls and the officials of the institution. They further pointed out that in case mail was censored, girls found methods of getting letters in and out of the institution without going through the superintendent's hands, and this not only made the censorship ineffective, but caused the girls to commit acts of deceit that were harmful to their characters. It is the opinion of the writer that the institution should reserve the right to censor all mail, and that both incoming and outgoing mail should pass through the hands of the superintendent. Girls in whom the superintendent has confidence should be told that, while as a matter of form their letters were opened in the superintendent's office, they were not read.

Visits to Inmates. Visits to inmates, except by near relatives, should not be encouraged, especially during the first part of their stay in the home. There should be regular hours for visits and twice a month or once a week at the most should be sufficient. If possible, arrangements should be made in advance so that all of the visits would not fall at the same hour. Unless the visitor is a person in whom the superintendent has complete confidence one of the officers of the home should be present during the visit.

Posting of Rules. As it should be the efforts of all to make the institution a real home for the girls, rules should not be posted. Upon admittance each girl should be furnished with a printed or typewritten copy of the rules and asked to familiarize herself with their provision.

Establishment of Loan Funds. Every maternity home should establish a revolving loan fund, which should be placed in the hands of the superintendent. The money in this fund should be available for loans to former inmates who are out of employment or in temporary need. Girls to whom loans are made should be required to repay the principal at the time agreed upon. The superintendent should make regular reports to the board of the loans and repayments.

Methods of Financing a Maternity Home. The following are the principal methods of financing the operating expenses of a maternity home:

(a) By regular appropriations from the city, county, or State, either made in a lump sum or *per diem* for each inmate.

(b) By admission fees from the inmates.

(c) By appropriations from community chests or other forms of organized charity in a community.

(d) By interest from endowments, real estate, or other accumulated funds.

(e) By gifts from regular contributors or members made on a monthly or annual basis.

(f) By bazaars, fairs, entertainments, etc., arranged by members of the boards or groups of women interested in the institution.

[197]

In some instances field secretaries are employed who make a regular canvass of the city, county, or State, and solicit subscriptions. These field secretaries are generally employed on a salary based upon the amount of their collections. In other instances, maternity homes are largely supported by fraternal or civic organizations as their contribution to the community welfare.

Budget of a Maternity Home. Every maternity home should adopt a budget at the commencement of each year and should live within the amount agreed upon as nearly as possible. The cost of operation will depend upon many factors. Number of inmates, character of work undertaken, suitability of the plant, food costs in the community, number and salaries of employees are factors which affect the operating expenses. Salaries differ widely in various communities. As a rule superintendents are paid from $100 to $150 per month; nurses from $90 to $125; matrons or housekeepers from $40 to $75; and case workers from $75 to $125. Room, board, and laundry are furnished in addition to the salaries. The case worker is generally furnished with an inexpensive automobile.

The following is a typical budget of a maternity home, occupying a modern building in an average community of the United States. It cares for an average of 25 girls and 15 babies, and has three regular employees, and a social worker who also serves another institution:

Salaries:		Per month
Superintendent	$110.00	
Matron	50.00	
Nurse	90.00	
Social worker (half-time)	50.00	
		$300.00
Food, 29 adults at average cost of $11 per month		319.00
Fuel, light, and water		80.00

BUDGET OF A MATERNITY HOME

One-half cost of operating automobile	15.00
Medical supplies	13.75
Clothing, dry goods, etc.	17.00
Insurance	10.00
Repairs	35.50
Household and laundry supplies	14.00
Miscellaneous expenses	19.00
Monthly total	$823.25
Annual budget	$9,879.00

APPENDIX

LIST OF PHILANTHROPIC MATERNITY HOMES FOR UNMARRIED MOTHERS IN THE UNITED STATES

ALABAMA

Mobile: Florence Crittenton Home, 8 Burt St.; ausp. N. F. C. M.; cap. 25 girls, 30 babies; hospital.

Birmingham: Women's Home and Hospital, 915 Montevallo Road, Route 3, Box 157 AA; ausp. S. A.; hospital.

ARIZONA

Phoenix: Florence Crittenton Home, 1022 E. Garfield St.; ausp. N. F. C. M.; cap. 25 girls, 25 babies; hospital.

ARKANSAS

Hot Springs: Florence Crittenton Home, 115 Crescent St.; ausp. N. F. C. M.; cap. 4 girls.

Little Rock: Florence Crittenton Home, 3600 West Eleventh St.; ausp. N. F. C. M.; cap. 30 girls, 20 babies; hospital.

CALIFORNIA

Los Angeles: Big Sisters' League, 2118 Trinity St.; cap. 15 girls, 25 children.

Florence Crittenton Home, 234 East Avenue 33; ausp. N. F. C. M.; cap. 30 girls, 25 babies; hospital.

Woman's Home and Hospital, 2670 N. Griffin Ave.; ausp. S. A.; cap. 20 girls, 15 babies; hospital.

Oakland: California Rescue Home, 1218 East 21st St.; ausp. Pacific Protective Society; venereally infected del. girls only; cap. 45 girls, 10 babies; hospital.

The Evangeline Booth Home and Hospital, 2794 Garden St.; ausp. S. A.; cap. 24 girls, 38 babies; hospital.

Sacramento: Peniel Rescue Home, Route 4, Box 750; cap. 40 girls, 25 babies; hospital.

San Francisco: Florence Crittenton Home, 376 20th Ave.; ausp. N. F. C. M.; cap. 20 girls, 15 babies.

Presbyterian Chinese Mission Home, 920 Sacramento St.; cap. 44 girls, 17 babies.

House of Friendship.

Women's Home and Hospital (Japanese), 1432 Laguna St.; ausp. S. A.; cap. 14 girls, 6 babies.

St. Elizabeth's.

COLORADO

Denver: Florence Crittenton Home, 4901 West Colfax; ausp. N. F. C. M.; cap. 50 girls, 50 babies; hospital.

Women's Home and Hospital, 1001 Jasmine St.; ausp. S. A.; cap. 25 girls, 25 babies; hospital.

Cottage Home, 427 Fairfax St.; ausp. W. C. T. U.; cap. 17 girls.

CONNECTICUT

Hartford: Gray Lodge, 391 Ann St. (protective agency).

St. Agnes' Home, Asylum Ave. and Steele Rd., West Hartford; ausp. R. C. Church; cap. 40 women, 198 children; hospital.

Women's Aid Society, 319 Barbour St.; cap. 12 girls, 12 children.

New Haven: Florence Crittenton Home, 1092 Campbell Ave., West Haven; ausp. N. F. C. M.; cap. 30 girls, 20 babies.

DELAWARE

Wilmington: Florence Crittenton Home, 506 West Fifth St.; ausp. N. F. C. M.; cap. 15 girls, 15 babies; hospital.

DISTRICT OF COLUMBIA

Washington: Florence Crittenton Home, 4759 Conduit Rd.; ausp. N. F. C. M.; cap. 45 girls, 40 babies; hospital.

House of Mercy, Rosemont Ave. and Klingle; ausp. P. E. Church; cap. 30 girl, 30 babies; hospital.

St. Ann's Infant Asylum and Maternity Hospital, 2300 K St., N. W.; ausp. R. C. Church; hospital.

FLORIDA

St. Petersburg: Florence Crittenton Home, 28th St. and 15th Ave., N.;

P. O. Box 3611; ausp. N. F. C. M.; cap. 12 girls, 12 babies; hospital.
Zephyrhills: Mizpah Rescue Home; cap. 10 girls, 10 babies; hospital.

GEORGIA

Atlanta: Florence Crittenton Home, 1061 Simpson St.; ausp. N. F. C. M.;
cap. 25 girls, 25 babies; hospital.
Macon: Tabernacle Rescue Home, 926 Montpelier Ave. cap. 12 girls, 12
children; hospital.
Savannah: Florence Crittenton Home, near Thunderbolt; ausp. N. F. C. M.;
cap. 20 girls, 15 babies; hospital.
Emergency Home, 309 East Boston St.; ausp. V. of A.; cap. 14 girls, 6
babies; hospital.

IDAHO

Boise: Women's Home and Hospital, 1617 N. 24th St.; ausp. S. A.; cap.
20 girls, 15 babies; hospital.

ILLINOIS

Chicago: Beulah Home and Maternity Hospital, 2144 North Clark St.; cap.
40 girls, 40 babies; hospital.
Florence Crittenton Home, 2615 Indiana Ave.; ausp. N. F. C. M.; cap.
20 girls, 15 babies.
Foundlings Home, cap. 25 girls.
St. Margaret's Home and Maternity Hospital, 2501 West Monroe St.;
ausp. R. C. Church; cap. 25 girls, 32 children.
St. Vincent's Infant and Maternity Hospital, 721 North La Salle St.;
ausp. R. C. Church; cap. 40 girls.
Sarah Hackett Stevenson Home, cap. 25 girls.
Women's Home and Hospital, 5040 Crawford Ave.; ausp. S. A.; cap. 105
girls and babies; hospital.
Hinsdale: Life Boat Rescue Home, Philipa and Sanford Sts.; cap. 14 girls,
30 babies.
Peoria: Florence Crittenton Home, 429 Richmond Ave.; ausp. N. F. C. M.;
cap. 25 girls, 25 babies; hospital.
Springfield: Springfield Redemption Home, 127-157 North Douglas Ave.;
cap. 30 girls, 20 babies; hospital.

INDIANA

Evansville: Vanderburgh Christian Home, 2215 Fulton Ave.; cap. 20 girls, 20 children; hospital.

Indianapolis: Florence Crittenton Home, 2044 North Illinois St.; ausp. N. F. C. M.; cap. 25 girls, 25 babies.

St. Elizabeth's Home, R. R. No. 5, Box 354; ausp. R C. Church.

South Bend: Florence Crittenton Circle, 549 Edgewater Drive; ausp. N. F. C. M.

Terre Haute: Beulah Rescue Home, R. F. D. Box 86; ausp. Pilgrim Holiness Church; cap. 15 girls, 16 babies; hospital.

Florence Crittenton Home, 1923 Poplar St.; ausp. N. F. C. M.; cap. 15 girls, 19 babies.

IOWA

Des Moines: St. Monica's Home, 1011 Park Ave.; ausp. House of Mercy (P. E. Church).

Benedict Home, 1611 27th St.; ausp. W. C. T. U.; cap. 28 girls, 10 babies; hospital.

Women's Home and Hospital, 3027 Indianola Rd.; ausp. S. A.; cap. 44 girls, 22 babies; hospital.

Dubuque: St. Theresa's Home.

Sioux City: Florence Crittenton Home, 1105 28th St.; ausp. N. F. C. M.; cap. 45 girls, 30 babies; hospital.

KANSAS

Lansing: Hope Cottage Rescue Home; ausp. United Brethren Church; cap. 8 girls, 9 babies.

Topeka: Florence Crittenton Home, 2601 Union Ave.; ausp. N. F. C. M.; cap. 15 girls, 10 babies; hospital.

Florence Crittenton Home for Colored Girls, 931 College Ave.; ausp. N. F. C. M.; cap. 12 girls, 10 babies; hospital.

Wichita: Women's Home and Hospital, 2050 Beal St.; ausp. S. A.; cap. 31 girls, 18 babies; hospital.

KENTUCKY

Covington: Wm. Booth Memorial Hospital, 323 East 2nd St.; ausp. S. A.; hospital.

Lexington: Florence Crittenton Home, 519 West 4th St.; ausp. N. F. C. M.; cap. 10 girls, 10 babies; hospital.
Louisville: Susan Speed Davis Home, 512 West Kentucky St.; ausp. S. A.; cap. 41 girls, 32 babies; hospital.

LOUISIANA

Lake Charles: Southwestern Training Home.
Monroe: Home of the Good Samaritan, Motor Route A, South; cap. 25 girls, 15 children.
New Orleans: Memorial Mercy Home, 815 Washington Ave.; ausp. M. E. Church South; cap. 40 girls, 40 children; hospital.
  Volunteers of America Maternity Home.
Shreveport: Hepozibah Home, 1530 Arlington St.; ausp. Union Mission Assn.; cap. 100 girls, 75 children; hospital.

MAINE

Bangor: Good Samaritan Home, 334 Union St.; cap. 35 girls, 15 babies; hospital.
Old Orchard: Harvey Memorial Florence Crittenton Circle, 6 Central Ave.; ausp. N. F. C. M. (summer work only for mothers and babies).
Portland: Temporary Home for Women and Children, 14 Prowsland St.; cap. 16 girls, 19 children.

MARYLAND

Baltimore: Florence Crittenton Home, 32nd St. and Chestnut Ave.; ausp. N. F. C. M.; cap. 40 girls, 40 babies.

MASSACHUSETTS

Boston: Evangeline Booth Home and Hospital, 202 West Newton St.; ausp. S. A.; cap. 31 girls, 26 babies; hospital.
  Florence Crittenton Home, 10 Perthshire Road, Brighton; 13 Bond St., Boston; ausp. N. F. C. M.; cap. 50 girls, 50 babies; hospital.
  House of Mercy, 244 Townsend St.; ausp. P. E. Church; cap. 21 girls, 14 babies; hospital.
  Talitha Cumi Maternity Home and Hospital, 215 Forest Hills St.; cap. 28 girls, 16 babies; hospital.
Lowell: Florence Crittenton Circle, Lowell Five Cent Bank Building; ausp. N. F. C. M.

New Bedford: Women's Reform and Relief Assn., 180 Allen St.; cap. 14
  girls, 2 babies.
New Bedford Children's Aid Society, 6 Eighth St.
Swampscott: Florence Crittenton Home, 145 Essex St.; ausp. N. F. C. M.;
  cap. 25 girls, 25 babies; hospital.
Worcester: Girls' Welfare Society, 5 Dudley Pl.; cap. 12 girls, 10 children.

MICHIGAN

Detroit: Booth Memorial Women's Home and Hospital, 130 West Grand
  Boulevard; ausp. S. A.; cap. 26 girls, 10 babies; hospital.
  Florence Crittenton Home, 583 East Elizabeth St.; ausp. N. F. C. M.; cap.
    190 girls, 190 babies; hospital.
  Williams House, 708 Charlotte Ave.; ausp. House of Mercy (P. E.
    Church); cap. 37 girls.
Grand Rapids: Evangeline Booth Home, 1215 East Fulton St.; ausp. S. A.;
  cap. 26 girls, 18 babies; hospital.
  Rest Cottage Rescue Home, 1041 East Fulton St.; cap. 26 girls, 11 babies.
Jackson: Florence Crittenton Home, 1603 Lansing Ave.; ausp. N. F. C. M.;
  cap. 30 girls, 20 babies.

MINNESOTA

Duluth: Bethel Home for Women and Children, 1230 East 9th St.; cap. 25
  girls, 30 children; hospital.
Minneapolis: Bethany Hospital, 3701 Bryant Ave.; cap. 50 girls, 35 babies;
  hospital.
  Lutheran Girl's Home, 1918 19th Ave., N. E.; ausp. Lutheran Church;
    cap. 36 girls, 36 babies; hospital.
  Scandinavian Home of Shelter, 2010 19th Ave., N. E.; cap. 19 girls, 26
    children.
St. Paul: Women's Home and Hospital, 1471 Como Ave.; ausp. S. A.; cap.
  45 girls, 30 babies; hospital.
  Union Gospel Mission House, 1245 North Hamline Ave.; cap. 22 girls,
    14 children; hospital.

MISSISSIPPI

Natchez: The King's Daughters Rescue Home, Cemetery Rd.; ausp. K. D.;
  cap. 25 girls, 25 babies; hospital.

LIST OF PHILANTHROPIC MATERNITY HOMES

MISSOURI

Kansas City: Florence Crittenton Home, 3003 Woodland Ave.; ausp. N. F. C. M.; 24 girls, 24 babies; hospital.

Florence Home for Colored Girls, 2446 Michigan Ave.; ausp. N. F. C. M.; cap. 30 girls, 30 babies; hospital.

Rest Cottage, 2905 Campbell St.; ausp. Church of the Nazarene; cap. 21 girls, 12 children.

St. Louis: Bethany Rescue Home, 4205 North 11th St.; cap. 25 girls and babies.

Hepzibah Rescue Home, 3014 Morgan St.

St. Louis Home and Mission of Redeeming Love, 4310 Enright Ave. (for colored girls).

Women's Home and Hospital, 3740 Marine Ave.; ausp. S. A.; cap. 25 girls, 34 babies; hospital.

MONTANA

Helena: Florence Crittenton Home, 22 Jefferson St.; ausp. N. F. C. M.; cap. 35 girls, 30 babies; hospital.

NEBRASKA

Milford: Nebraska Industrial Home; State institution for unmarried mothers and babies; cap. 60 girls; hospital.

Omaha: Women's Home and Hospital, 1702 Grace St.; ausp. S. A.; cap. 25 girls, 34 babies; hospital.

NEW JERSEY

Atlantic City: Florence Crittenton Home, 1916 Adriatic Ave.; ausp. N. F. C. M.; cap. 15 girls, 10 babies; hospital.

Jersey City: Door of Hope, 503 Garfield Ave.; ausp. S. A.; cap. 20 girls, 14 babies; hospital.

St. Katherine's Home, 32 Reservoir Ave.; ausp. House of Mercy (P. E. Church); cap. 12 girls, 12 babies.

Newark: Florence Crittenton Home, 206 Ogden St.; ausp. N. F. C. M.; cap. 30 girls, 20 babies; hospital.

Ocean Grove: Florence Crittenton Home, 82 Heck Ave.; ausp. N. F. C. M.; (summer work only).

THE CARE OF THE UNMARRIED MOTHER

Patterson: Florence Crittenton Home, 700 East 18th St.; ausp. N. F. C. M.; cap. 25 girls, 29 babies; hospital.

Princeton: Florence Crittenton Circle (protective work only).

Scotch Plains: Union Rescue Home, 56 Plainsfield Ave.; cap. 35 girls and children.

Trenton: Florence Crittenton Home, 1212 Edgewood Ave.; ausp. N. F. C. M.; cap. 15 girls, 10 babies; hospital.

Mary Faith Home.

NEW YORK

Binghamton: The Refuge, 84 Fairview Ave.; cap. 10 girls, 10 babies; hospital.

Brooklyn: Welcome House for Girls, 139 Bainbridge St.; cap. 15 girls, 6 children.

Buffalo: Brent House, 12 St. John's Pl.; ausp. House of Mercy (P. E. Church.

Ingleside Home, 70 Harvard Pl.; cap. 42 girls, 27 children; hospital.

Salvation Army Home and Hospital, 69 Cottage St.; ausp. S. A.; cap. 27 girls, 24 babies; hospital.

St. Mary's Infants Home and Hospital; ausp. R. C. Church.

Mamaroneck: St. Michael's Home, 53 Mt. Pleasant Ave.; ausp. House of Mercy (P. E. Church); cap. 45 girls.

New York City: Booth Memorial Home and Hospital, 312 East 15th St.; ausp. S. A.; cap. 23 girls, 21 babies; hospital.

Florence Crittenton Home, 427 West 21st; ausp. N. F. C. M.; cap. 35 girls.

Heartsease Home for Women and Babies, 413 East 51st; cap. 12 girls, 6 babies.

Katy Ferguson Home and Sojourner Truth House, 162 West 130th St. (colored girls).

Lakeview Home, Arrochar, Staten Island; a home for Jewish unmarried mothers.

Ozanam Home for Friendless Women of Brooklyn, 40 Concord St., Brooklyn; cap. 100 girls.

Seventeen Beekman Place, 17 Beekman Pl.; cap. 24 girls, 6 babies.

Washington Square Home for Friendless Girls, 9 West 8th; cap. 15 girls.

Rochester: Rochester Community Home for Girls, 293 Troup St.; cap. 10 girls, 7 babies.

LIST OF PHILANTHROPIC MATERNITY HOMES

Tarrytown: St. Faith's House, 53 Broadway; ausp. House of Mercy (P. E. Church); cap. 20 girls, 15 babies.

Utica: Door of Hope, 1020 Mathews Ave.; cap. 12 girls, 12 babies.

Valhalla: St. Faith's House; ausp. House of Mercy (P. E. Church); cap. 45 girls.

NORTH CAROLINA

Asheville: Compton Rescue Home; cap. 18 girls and babies.

Candler: Lindley Home, Route 2, Box 49; cap. 25 girls and babies.

Charlotte: Florence Crittenton Home, 513 North McDowell St.; ausp. N. F. C. M.; cap. 35 girls, 25 babies; hospital.

Greensboro: Rest Cottage, 812 Haywood St.; cap. 12 girls, 12 babies; hospital.

Wilmington: Women's Home and Hospital, 110 Orange St.; ausp. S. A.; cap. 45 girls and babies; hospital.

NORTH DAKOTA

Fargo) Florence Crittenton Home, 713 South 13th St.; ausp. N. F. C. M.; cap. 50 girls, 40 babies; hospital.

North Dakota House of Mercy, 1505 Fifth Ave., S.; ausp. Norwegian Lutheran Church; cap. 16 girls, 14 babies; hospital.

OHIO

Akron: Florence Crittenton Home, 51 Cotter Ave.; ausp. N. F. C. M.; cap. 15 girls, 10 babies.

Canton: Bethshan Home, 1612 Harrisburg Rd., N. E.; cap. 14 girls, 9 babies; hospital.

Cincinnati: Catherine Booth Home, 836 Beecher St.; ausp. S. A.; cap. 28 girls, 25 babies; hospital.

Evangeline Booth Home, 712 West 6th St.; ausp. S. A.; cap. 25 girls, 17 babies; hospital (for colored girls).

Maple Knoll Hospital and Home for the Friendless, R. F. D. 5, Box 327; cap. 50 girls, 50 babies; hospital.

Rescue Home (God's Bible School), Riaggold, Young and Channing Sts.

Cleveland: Florence Crittenton Home, 523 Eddy Rd.; ausp. N. F. C. M.; cap. 20 girls, 20 babies; hospital.

Maternity Home, 5905 Kinsman Rd.; cap. 35 girls, 33 babies; hospital.

Mary B. Talbert Home, 2215 East 40th St.; ausp. S. A.; cap. 25 girls, 25 babies; hospital (for colored girls).

Salvation Army Home, 5905 Kinsman Rd.; ausp. S. A.; cap. 35 girls, 33 babies; hospital.

St. Anne's Maternity Home; cap. 75 girls and babies.

The Retreat, 2697 Woodhill Ave.; cap. 18 girls, 18 babies; hospital.

Columbus: Florence Crittenton Home, 1166 East Main St.; ausp. N. F. C. M.; cap. 30 girls, 20 babies; hospital.

Friends Rescue Home, North Hague Ave.; cap. 17 girls; hospital.

Mary Price Home for Colored Girls, 164 North 22nd St.

Dayton: Door of Hope, 542 St. Joseph Ave.; city institution; cap. 16 girls, 6 children.

East Akron: Florence Crittenton Home, Box 257, Route No. 1; ausp. N. F. C. M.; cap. 15 girls, 10 babies.

Glendale: Hope Cottage, Sharon Ave.; cap. 11 girls, 4 babies.

Portsmouth: Hopedale Rescue Home, 4228 Milldale Rd.; cap. 10 girls, 10 children; hospital.

Toledo: Florence Crittenton Home, 737 Ontario St.; ausp. N. F. C. M.; cap. 20 girls, 15 babies.

Youngstown: Florence Crittenton Home, 1161 East Madison Ave.; ausp. N. F. C. M.; cap. 20 girls, 15 babies; hospital.

OKLAHOMA

Oklahoma City: Holmes Home of Redeeming Love, 54th and Portland Sts.; cap. 55 girls, 50 babies; hospital.

OREGON

Portland: Florence Crittenton Home, 955 East Glisan St.; ausp. N. F. C. M.; cap. 25 girls, 25 babies; hospital.

Louise Home, Box 260, Route 9; ausp. Pac. Protective Soc.; cap. 120 girls, 120 babies; hospital.

White Shield Home and Hospital, 565 Mayfair Ave.; ausp. S. A.; cap. 32 girls, 39 babies; hospital.

PENNSYLVANIA

Allison Park: Zoah Home, Butler Pike; cap. 15 girls, 20 babies.

Erie: Florence Crittenton Home, 501 Holland St.; ausp. N. F. C. M.; cap. 15 girls, 10 babies; hospital.

Pittsburgh: Florence Crittenton Home, 535 South Aiken St.; ausp. N. F.
C. M.; cap. 20 girls, 20 babies.

Salvation Army Home, 108 Mead Ave., Bellevue; ausp. S. A.; cap. 19
girls, 30 babies; hospital.

Christian Home for Women, 1423 Liverpool St.; cap. 30 girls, 10 babies.

Roselia Foundling Asylum and Maternity Hospital, Clift and Manila Sts.;
ausp. R. C. Church; cap. 68 girls, 109 children; hospital.

Philadelphia: Florence Crittenton Home, 139 Queen Lane; ausp. N. F.
C. M.; cap. 15 girls, 15 babies; hospital.

Hebrew Sheltering Arms, Wissahickon Ave. and School Lane, Germantown;
cap. 65 girls and children.

Salvation Army Home, 5415 Lansdowne Ave.; ausp. S. A.; cap. 27 girls,
31 babies; hospital.

Sheltering Arms of the P. E. Church, West School and Gypsy Lane, Germantown; cap. 23 girls, 21 children.

St. Vincent's Home and Maternity Hospital, 70th St. and Woodland Ave.;
ausp. R. C. Church; cap. 25 girls.

Scranton: Florence Crittenton Home, 712 Harrison Ave.; ausp. N. F. C. M.;
cap. 15 girls, 15 babies.

St. Joseph's Foundling Home and Maternity Hospital, 1850 Adams Ave.;
ausp. R. C. Church; cap. 260 girls and children.

Upland: Temporary Shelter for Women, "The Gables," 6th and Main Sts.;
cap. 26 girls, 25 children.

Wilkesbarre: Florence Crittenton Home, 23 Park Ave.; ausp. N. F. C. M.;
cap. 25 girls, 20 babies; hospital.

Williamsport: Florence Crittenton Home, 673 Campbell St.; ausp. N. F.
C. M.; cap. 12 girls, 10 babies; hospital.

RHODE ISLAND

Providence: Providence Rescue Home and Mission, 30 Benefit St.; cap. 13
girls and children.

SOUTH CAROLINA

Charleston: Florence Crittenton Home, 368 President St. (temporary address); ausp. N. F. C. M.; cap. 60 girls, 40 babies; hospital.

Columbia: Door of Hope, 1516 Calhoun St.; cap. 40 girls, 25 children;
hospital.

Greenville: Emma Moss Booth Memorial Hospital, Vardry Heights; ausp.
S. A.; cap. 53 girls, 56 babies; hospital.

SOUTH DAKOTA

Sioux Falls: Lutheran House of Mercy, 407 North Spring Ave.; ausp. Norwegian Lutheran Church; cap. 14 girls, 14 babies.

TENNESSEE

Chattanooga: Florence Crittenton Home, 500 Thirty-third St.; ausp. N. F.
C. M.; cap. 12 girls, 10 babies; hospital.

Nashville: Florence Crittenton Home, 701 South 5th St., East; ausp. N. F.
C. M.; cap. 40 girls, 30 babies; hospital.

Memphis: Bethany Training Home, 901 Chelsea Ave.; cap. 20 girls, 20
babies.

Beulah Training Home, 1051 Pearce St.; cap. 30 girls, 20 babies; hospital.

Ella Oliver Refuge, 903 Walker Ave.; cap. 12 girls, 12 babies; hospital.

TEXAS

Arlington: Berachah Home, Drawer 38; cap. 60 girls, 60 children; hospital.

Dallas: Virginia K. Johnson Maternity Home.

El Paso: Home for Girls.

Ft. Worth: Maternity Home, 2710 Avenue J; ausp. V. of A.; cap. 8 girls,
3 babies.

Houston: Florence Crittenton Home, 3119 Carolina Ave.; ausp. N. F. C. M.;
cap. 15 girls, 10 babies.

Pilot Point: Rest Cottage; ausp. Church of the Nazarene; Cap. 50 girls, 30
children; hospital.

San Antonio: Women's Home and Hospital, 4019 Broadway; ausp. S. A.;
cap. 30 girls, 22 babies; hospital.

Mission Home and Training School, 223 South San Saba St.; cap. 64 girls,
42 babies.

UTAH

Ogden: Florence Crittenton Home, 2544 Porter Ave.; ausp. N. F. C. M.;
cap. 10 girls, 10 babies.

VERMONT

Burlington: Elizabeth Lund Home, 346 Shelburne Rd.; cap. 14 girls, 20
babies; hospital.

LIST OF PHILANTHROPIC MATERNITY HOMES

VIRGINIA

Alexandria: National Florence Crittenton Mission, 408 Duke St.

Clifton Station: Ivakota Farms; ausp. N. F. C. M.; cap. 125 girls and babies; hospital.

Lynchburg: Florence Crittenton Home, 1803 Taylor St.; ausp. N. F. C. M.; cap. 20 girls, 15 babies; hospital.

Norfolk: Florence Crittenton Home, 771 52nd St.; ausp. N. F. C. M.; 30 girls, 20 babies; hospital.

Richmond: Spring Street Home, 601 Spring St.; cap. 20 girls, 20 children; hospital.

Women's Home and Hospital, 2701 Fifth Ave., Highland Park; ausp. S. A.; cap. 20 girls, 20 babies; hospital.

Roanoke: Women's Home and Hospital, 521 Salem Ave.; ausp. S. A.; cap. 12 girls, 6 babies; hospital.

WASHINGTON

Everett: Washington Girl's Home, 4220 South Colby Ave.; ausp. Pac. Protective Society; cap. 45 girls, 41 babies; hospital.

Seattle: Florence Crittenton Home, 9236 Renton Ave.; ausp. N. F. C. M.; cap. 30 girls, 25 babies; hospital.

Lebanon Home, 1110 West 65th St.; cap. 15 girls, 10 babies.

Spokane: Florence Crittenton Home, 707 North Cedar St.; ausp. N. F. C. M.; cap. 20 girls, 15 babies; hospital.

Women's Home and Hospital, 3422 Garland Ave.; ausp. S. A.; cap. 46 girls, 5 babies; hospital.

WEST VIRGINIA

Wheeling: Florence Crittenton Home, Elm Grove; ausp. N. F. C. M.; cap. 35 girls, 25 babies; hospital.

WISCONSIN

Green Bay: St. Mary's Mothers and Infants Home; ausp. R. C. Church; cap. 40 girls, 60 children; hospital.

Wauwatosa: Martha Washington Home, 6304 Cedar St.; ausp. S. A.; cap. 45 girls, 31 children; hospital.

FORMS FOR MATERNITY HOMES

EXHIBIT 1

ADMISSION RECORD

_____MATERNITY HOME

Name _____Hosp. No._____

Date application _____Full name parents _____

Who applied—how_____ Residence parents_____

Entrance____._____ Age_____

Mother working_____ When do you expect baby?_____

Source information_____ Birthplace_____

Residence_____ Religion_____

Education_____ Occupation_____

Wages_____ Remarks_____

Have you ever been married?_____Is this your first pregnancy?_____

I hereby agree to remain in the home until I have been discharged by the management, and
I agree to comply cheerfully with the rules of the Home.

Sign_____

EXHIBIT 2

CURRENT RECORD

Entered _____No.

Left _____

Name _____

Married_____ Single_____

Age_____..   _____ Birthplace_____

Came in through?_____ Date_____

Residence at time of admittance_____

Past Residence _____

Child's Name _____ Date Birth_____

Wgt. _____ Sex_____ Condition at birth_____

Doctor on case_____ Left_____

PARENTS

Father_____ Mother_____

Age_____ Residence_____

Occupation_____ Birthplace_____

Grade left school_____Last mens._____Family defects_____

Tb._____ Soc. Dis._____Insan._____Age left school_____

Physical cond._____ Age began work_____

Mentality_____ Religion_____

[215]

THE CARE OF THE UNMARRIED MOTHER

Occupation_____ Wages_____
Employer_____ Address_____
Time employed _____
Sex Instruction_____ Age first sex offence_____
Later sex offences_____
Men involved _____

Court history _____
_____
_____
_____

Other agencies interested _____
_____
_____

Date report C. E._____
_____

Father of child_____ Age_____
Address_____ M. or S._____
Occupation_____ Religion_____
Nationality _____
Parents _____ Physical Cond._____
Residence _____ Intemperate?_____

Institutional record _____
_____
_____
_____

Friend to be notified in emergency_____
_____
_____

Kinship_____ Name_____
Age_____ Address_____
Occupation_____ Ch._____
Circumstances (Girl's Story)_____
_____
_____
_____

Circumstances (Any other source)_____
_____
_____
_____

Environment and recreation_____
_____
_____

FORMS FOR MATERNITY HOMES

HISTORY OF GIRL DURING STAY IN HOME

Industrial Efficiency _____

_____

Behavior_____ Lying_____ Stealing_____
Cruelty _____Sex perversions_____
Any others (specify) _____

_____

_____

Disciplinary history _____

_____

_____

_____

PERSONALITY MAKEUP (Please underscore such traits as individual has).
Restless, quiet, indolent, industrious, responsive, easily-influenced, obedient, selfish,
gets along with others hypersuggestible, independent, excitable, temper tantrums,
hypersensitive, seclusive, impulsive, neurotic, easily discouraged, egotistic, individual-
istic, inconsiderate, unappreciative, weak-willed, sluggish, lacking in ambition,
suspicious, self-centred, sullen, others (specify)

Disposition of girl_____

_____

Disposition of child_____

_____

Subsequent History _____

_____

_____

_____

EXHIBIT 3

HISTORY AND LABOR RECORD

Hospital _____Date _____
Name_____ Address_____ Dr._____
Age_____ Race_____ Occupation_____
S. M. W. Years_____ Gravida_____
Family History—TBC_____ Epilepsy_____
Feeblemindedness _____

Previous illness or accidents_____ _____

Give dates _____

[217]

THE CARE OF THE UNMARRIED MOTHER

G. C.—Syphilis _____Date last small-pox vacc._____
Menstruation: First begun _____ Frequency_____
Pain_____ Duration_____ Amount_____
Marriage _____Husband's Health_____
Children: No._____ Ages_____ Wt. at b._____
No. living_____ Health_____
No. dead_____ Cause_____
Character of previous pregnancies, labors and puerperiums_____
_____
_____
Miscarriages: No._____ State of gestation_____
Cause _____
Last Menstruation, first day_____ Quickening_____
Estimated conf._____ Nausea and vomiting_____
Headache_____ Edema_____ Leucorrhea_____
Urine_____ Bowels_____ Miscellaneous_____

PHYSICAL EXAMINATION

Date_____ Measurements_____
Sp._____ Cr._____ Tr._____ Outlet_____ C. D._____ C. V._____
Eyes_____ Teeth_____ Tonsils_____
Thyroid_____ Nodes_____ Breasts_____
Nipples_____ Secretion_____ Heart_____
Lungs_____ Spine_____ Abdomen_____
Fetal Heart_____ Presentation_____ Position_____
Extremities_____ Vaginal_____ Rectal_____
Smears_____ Wass._____ Hemoglobin_____

LABOR RECORD

Date_____ Blood pressure_____
Urinalysis_____Presentation and position_____
Labor began_____ ended_____ Examinations_____
Vaginal—No._____ Rectal—No._____
Delivery: Anesthetic—kind_____ How long_____
Spontaneous_____ Operative—kind_____
Lacerations_____ Repaired_____ Hemorrhage_____
C. c. estimate_____ Placenta_____ Spontaneous_____
Manual_____ Medications—time_____ Complications_____

(Note: The reverse of this sheet should contain space for daily record of condition of patient.)

APPENDIX

EXHIBIT 4

POST-PARTUM AND NEWBORN RECORD

POST-PARTUM EXAMINATION

Date_____ Number days post-partum_____
Breasts_____ Nipples_____ Uterus—Corpus_____
Position_____ Size_____ Cervix_____
Perineum—Lacerations or repairs healed_____
Urinalysis _____ Blood Pressure_____
Has patient had any elevation of temperature during the puerperium?_____
Explain _____

NEWBORN RECORD

Date _____ Name _____
Mother's Name_____ Time of Birth _____
Sex_____ Weight_____ Temperature_____
Month of gestation_____ Treatment of eyes_____ Cord_____
Cord off _____ Umbilicus—hernia_____
General physical condition_____ Anomalies, injuries_____
Evidence of venereal disease_____ Feeding—breast-fed—how often_____
Nurses well_____ If not breast-fed, why?_____ Artificial feeding_____
Sleep_____ Skin_____
Stools—No. per day_____ Character_____

EXHIBIT 5

RECORD TO BE SENT TO AND FROM GENERAL HOSPITAL WHERE CONFINEMENT TAKES PLACE

From _____ Maternity Home
To _____ Hospital
Name _____ Age _____
Prenatal Care—Where given_____ How long_____
Previous Pregnancies_____ Spontaneous_____ Instrumental_____
Complications_____ Miscarriages_____ Stillbirths_____
Expected Confinement_____ Last Menses_____ Life felt_____
Physical Exam._____ Weight_____ Teeth_____ Thyroid_____
General Remarks _____

Heart_____ Lungs_____
Breasts _____ Nipples_____
Pelvic Measurements_____ Presentation_____
Extremities _____
Examination—Vaginal _____ Rectal_____
Urinalysis_____ Date_____ Blood Pressure_____
Smear_____ Wasserman_____ Haemoglobin_____ TBC_____

THE CARE OF THE UNMARRIED MOTHER

Remarks _____

_____

_____

_____

_____ (Perforate) _____

To _____ Maternity Home

From _____ Hospital

Name _____ Address _____

Delivered _____ Spontaneous _____ Instrumental _____

Complications _____ Lacerations _____

Repair _____ Hemorrhage _____ Hours in Labor _____

No. Days in Bed _____ Date Discharged _____

Smear _____ Wasserman _____

Condition on Discharge _____

Baby—Sex _____ Weight at Birth _____

Term _____ Premature _____ Month of gestation _____

Abnormalities _____

Conditions on Discharge _____ Weight _____

Feeding on Discharge _____

Remarks _____

(If patient was admitted directly to General Hospital please fill in the following)

General Condition previous to delivery _____

Heart _____ Lungs _____ Kidneys _____

Is this the first child? _____

[220]

INDEX

INDEX

INDEX

INDEX

TITLES IN THIS SERIES

10 *Risks for the Single Woman in the City, An Anthology of Studies by Late Nineteenth-Century Reformers*. David J. and Sheila M. Rothman, eds. New York, 1986

11 *Saving Babies: Children's Bureau Studies of Infant Mortality, 1913–1917*. David J. and Sheila M. Rothman, eds. New York, 1986

12 *The Sheppard-Towner Act, the Record of the Hearings*. David J. and Sheila M. Rothman, eds. New York, 1986

13 *Women in Prison, 1834–1928, An Anthology of Pamphlets from the Progressive Movement*. David J. and Sheila M. Rothman, eds. New York, 1986

14 Azel Ames, Jr., *Sex in Industry: A Plea for the Working Girl*, Boston, 1875

15 Robert South Barrett, *The Care of the Unmarried Mother*, Alexandria, 1929

16 Elizabeth Blackwell, M.D., *The Laws of Life, with Special Reference to the Physical Education of Girls*, New York, 1852

17 Alida C. Bower and Ruth S. Bloodgood, *Institutional Treatment of Delinquent Boys*, Washington, D.C., 1935–36

18 New York Assembly, *The Girls of the Department Store*, New York, 1895

19 Committee on the Infant and Preschool Child, *Nursery Education*, New York, 1931

20 Robert Latou Dickinson and Lura Beam, *The Single Woman: A Medical Study in Sex Education*, Baltimore, 1934

21 G. V. Hamilton, M.D., *A Research in Marriage*, New York, 1929

22 Elizabeth Harrison, *A Study of Child Nature from the Kindergarten Standpoint*, Chicago, 1909

23 Orie Latham Hatcher, *Rural Girls in the City for Work*, Richmond, 1930

24 William Healy, Augusta F. Bronner, et al., *Reconstructing Behavior in Youth*, New York, 1929

25 Henry H. Hibbs, Jr., *Infant Mortality: Its Relation to Social and Industrial Conditions*, New York, 1916

26 *The Juvenile Court Record*, Chicago, 1900, 1901

27 Mary A. Livermore, *What Shall We Do With Our Daughters?* Boston, 1883

28 *Massachusetts Society for the Prevention of Cruelty to Children: First Ten Annual Reports*, Boston, 1882

29 Maude E. Miner, *Slavery of Prostitution: A Plea for Emancipation*, New York, 1916

30 Maud Nathan, *The Story of an Epoch-Making Movement*, New York, 1926

31 National Florence Crittenton Mission, *Fourteen Years' Work Among "Erring Girls,"* Washington, D.C., 1897

32 New York Milk Committee, *Reducing Infant Mortality in the Ten Largest Cities in the United States*, New York, 1912

33 James Orton, ed., *The Liberal Education of Women: The Demand and the Method*, New York, 1873

34 Margaret Reeves, *Training Schools for Delinquent Girls*, New York, 1929

35 Ben L. Reitman, M.D., *The Second Oldest Profession*, New York, 1931

36 John Dale Russell and Associates, *Vocational Education*, Washington, D.C., 1938

37 William H. Slingerland, *Child Welfare Work in California*, New York, 1916

38 William H. Slingerland, *Child Welfare Work in Pennsylvania*, New York, 1917

39 *Documents Relative to the House of Refuge, Instituted by the Society for the Reformation of Juvenile Delinquents in the City of New York, in 1824*, New York, 1832

40 George S. Stevenson, M.D., and Geddes Smith, *Child Guidance Clinics*, New York, 1934

41 Henry Winfred Thurston, *Delinquency and Spare Time*, New York, 1918

42 U.S. National Commission on Law Observance and Enforcement, *Report on Penal Institutions, Probation and Parole*, Washington, D.C., 1931

43 Miriam Van Waters, *Parents on Probation*, 1927

44 Ira S. Wile, M.D., *The Sex Life of the Unmarried Adult*, New York, 1934

45 Helen Leland Witmer, *Psychiatric Clinics for Children*, New York, 1940

46 Young Women's Christian Association, *First Ten Annual Reports, 1871–1880*, New York, 1871–1880